Beat around the Bush

Karley Brenna

Beat around the Bush

Copyright © 2024 by Karley Brenna

All rights reserved.

No part of this book may be reproduced in any form or by any electronic or mechanical means, including information storage and retrieval systems, without written permission from the author, except for the use of brief quotations in a book review.

This is a work of fiction. Any names, characters, places, brands, media, and incidents are either the products of the author's imagination and used in a fictitious manner. Any resemblance to actual people, places, or events is purely coincidental and fictional.

Do not copy, loan, sell, or redistribute.

Paperback ISBN: 979-8-9888184-2-7

Edited by: Bobbi Maclaren

Cover: Dirty Girl Designs by Ali Clemons

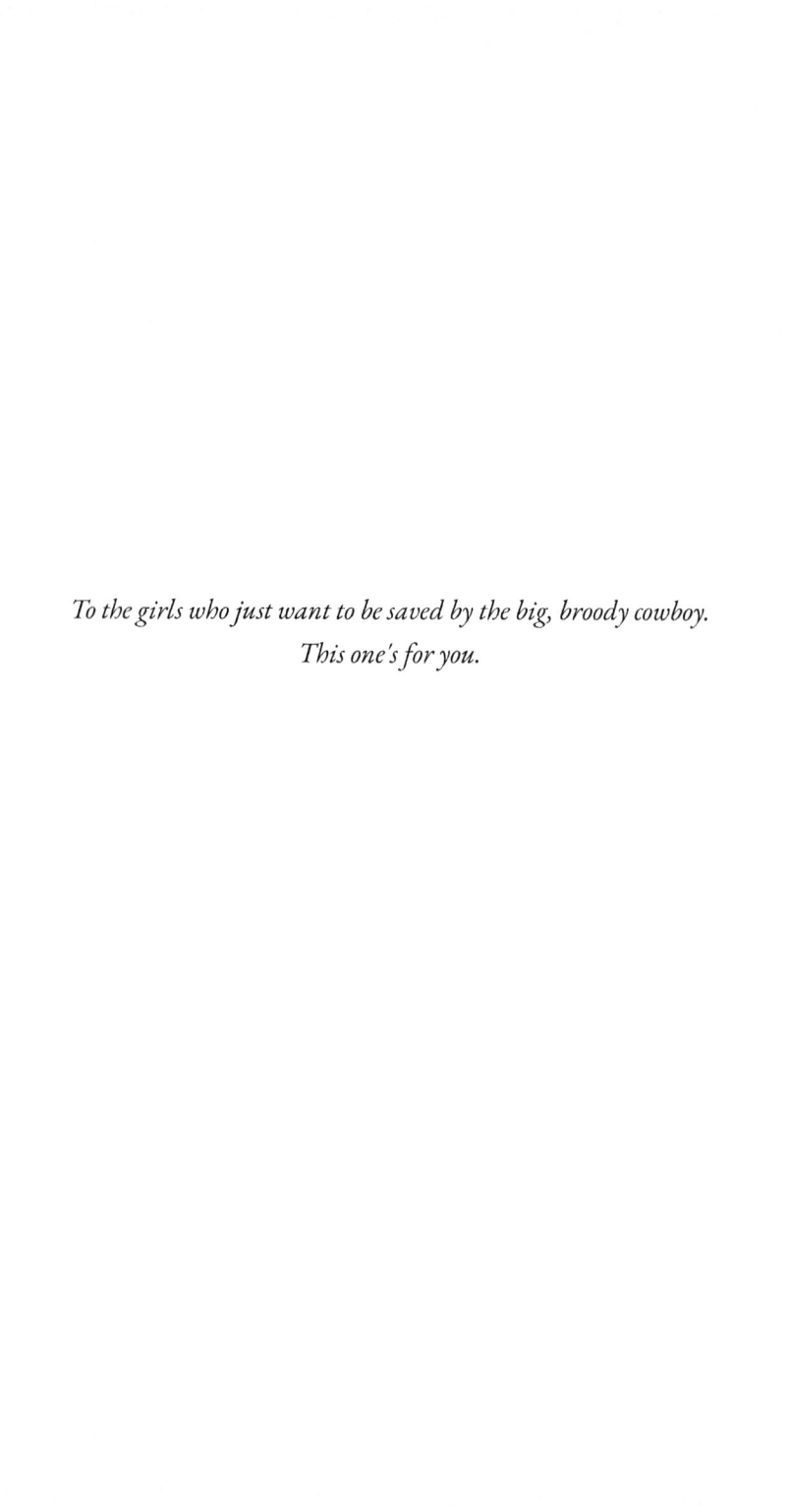

To the girls who just want to be saved by the big, broody cowboy.
This one's for you.

Important Note

Dear reader,

Please note that there is particular content and situations within these pages that may be triggering to some people. Some of these may be spoilers for certain scenes, so read this list at your own discretion:

-On page violence
-Stalking
-Strong language
-Sexually explicit content
-Mention of cheating (not by either of the main characters)
-Mention of divorce (not by either of the main characters)
-Minor car accident

*"You see, in this world, there's two kinds of people, my friend –
those with loaded guns, and those who dig. You dig."*
– Clint Eastwood

1

OAKLEY

The sound of metal crunching filled the car as my body was thrust forward against the seat belt. I cursed, slamming my foot on the brake despite my car already being stopped due to the truck now attached to my front bumper.

Shifting to park, I took a minute to catch my breath. I'd been so lost in thought about my parents that I hadn't seen the taillights until I was right on top of them. The rain pelting down didn't help, making visibility damn near nonexistent.

I knew it hadn't been a good idea to get groceries in this storm, but as most rentals come, the fridge was empty and I needed food. I couldn't keep eating fast food as that was all I'd done throughout the entire drive to this town in the middle of nowhere. I hadn't had time to do a full grocery trip because I'd been searching for a job since I arrived.

When I left Denver, I had no destination in mind, but halfway through my drive, I'd tried to find the nearest Taco Bell on my maps app, and oddly, Bell Buckle had popped up in the list. While there was clearly no Taco Bell in this town, the name was... somewhat close? Regardless, the name sounded cute, so I clicked it, and well, the rest was history.

Knuckles rapped on the window and I jumped, my hand shooting to my chest. Unbuckling my seat belt, I opened the door and stepped out.

"Are you alright?" the man asked, stepping back to give me space. It was dark despite the light from our headlights and the rain was coming down, making my ability to see his features almost nonexistent.

"I'm so sorry about your truck. I couldn't see very well with the storm and it's dark and I've never been very good at driving at night and-" He held a hand up to stop me.

He bent down slightly so we were eye level, his hood pulling back a little with the movement. Even with the little bit of light, I could see the hazel of his eyes shining, the color reminding me of the forest floor. "Are you okay?"

I managed a nod. "I'm okay, but your truck-"

"I don't care about the truck. You hit me pretty hard. Did you hit your head or anything? Are you feeling alright?"

Was he serious? I just slammed into his bumper and he didn't care? The man clearly wasn't from the city. Any other person would be filled with rage at the damage done.

Speaking of damage, I glanced over to where my front end was connected to his vehicle. My hood had slid right under his bumper, seemingly causing no damage to his truck. My car, on the other hand, had a dented hood.

Bringing my gaze back to him, I nodded again. "I feel fine. Do you want my insurance?" Before he could reply, I turned back to my car to reach in for my wallet, but a rough hand grabbed my elbow. Despite the cold, his skin was warm against mine. I'd forgotten my jacket at the rental when I rushed out the door to try and beat the worst of the storm.

I looked back at him, doing my best to ignore our point of contact. "No." He dropped my arm. "Don't need to involve insurance, unless you want to. My truck's fine. I can pay for the damages on your-"

"That's not necessary," I interrupted. Now I knew he couldn't be serious. I hit him, and he was offering to pay for the damages on my car?

My car was an old piece of junk anyway. If it was that bad, I'd just sell it for parts and use whatever money I had to buy a different vehicle.

My hair was dripping from the rain, droplets falling down my face as I tried to think of a way to get out of here. Hooking my hair behind my ears, I took a step back, gesturing to my car. "I should get home, I have groceries-"

"Yeah," he replied before I could finish my sentence. "Let me just take a look under your hood, make sure everything's fine." He was offering it, phrasing it more like a question.

This entire situation was so beyond awkward, I just wanted to leave. I already felt like an idiot rear-ending him. He probably thought I was just another tourist who didn't know how to drive unless the sun was out.

To give him a sense of peace before we parted ways, I agreed. "Sure. That'd be nice, just in case."

He eyed me before giving a slow nod. He didn't move, so I finally spoke up. "Aren't you going to check?"

"Need you to reverse it a few feet."

Embarrassment flooded my cheeks as I remembered my hood was currently pinned under his truck.

"Right," I muttered before getting in my car, shifting into reverse, and backing up a few feet. The front of my car lifted a few inches as I slipped out from under his bumper. I looked over my steering wheel to assess my hood. With how bad it sounded, there was surprisingly little to no damage, aside from the dent.

I could live with a dent. I just needed my car.

After shifting back into park, I got out, closing the door behind me as he lifted the hood, his fingers finding the clasp under the metal like he did this often. He was wearing a black Carhartt, but even under the jacket, I could tell he was built.

I should not be checking out the guy I just fucking slammed my car into.

Averting my gaze, I wiped the water from my cheeks. The rain was deafening, drowning out the sounds of our engines idling. He closed the hood, turning to me. "Looks fine from what I can see right now. I'd take it to a shop, though. There's one in town, if you're staying around here. They open at eight a.m. tomorrow. North State Auto," he said, having to raise his voice over the downpour.

"Thanks. I'll give them a call in the morning." There was no way I would be calling them. I barely had enough money in my account to cover the groceries I just bought. No way was I paying a mechanic to lie about some problem on my car and upcharge the hell out of me.

"You're sure you're okay?" he asked again.

"Yep. Get home safe," I clipped, turning to slip back into my car. He was still standing there when I closed my door and cranked up the heater.

I grabbed a few napkins from my center console and watched as he disappeared into his truck while I patted my face dry and wrung out the ends of my soaked hair. These storms in the west were no joke. I knew that from having grown up in Colorado, but no matter how long I'd been around them, I'd never been able to get used to them.

Seeing that he wasn't pulling away, I shifted into drive, and pulled around his truck, heading down the road. I watched in my rearview mirror as he continued on his way. Releasing a deep breath of air, I headed in the direction of my rental.

I internally told myself not to think of my mother or the fact that my dad hadn't stopped calling me since I left Denver. I could deal with all of that later. Right now, I just needed to make it back to the rental I was calling home, unload these groceries, scarf down some food, and get a good night's sleep before my interview tomorrow.

The rest could wait.

2

Lennon

Grabbing a clean travel mug from the cabinet, I poured myself a cup of coffee. Black, just how I liked it. With how shitty my night went, I'd need all the caffeine I could get today.

I'd tossed and turned for hours. Everytime I closed my eyes, all I saw was amber hair and eyes so green I thought they were fake. The dim light of the headlights did little to hide her.

She'd looked so damn pale when she got out of her car, a tremble in her hands as she rambled. I couldn't give two shits less about my damn truck at that moment. Knowing if she was alright was the only thought on my mind at the time.

These storms weren't for the weak, which led me to wonder why she was even out in it in the first place. I'd been driving home from Tumbleweed Feed, the only feed store in town, when she'd hit my truck so hard at the four-way stop that it jerked forward a few inches.

My '78 GMC K15 didn't budge easy, but man, had she slammed into it. She had to have been looking at her phone or something and not realized there was a stop sign. I was just thankful she hit *me*, because if she had ended up going through the intersection without looking, someone could have hit her.

I pushed the thought of someone smashing into the side of her car away and downed the rest of my coffee, then refilled my mug to the rim. After grabbing my baseball cap off the kitchen table, I headed out the door, locking it behind me.

Typically, I tried to get to the feed store before whoever was scheduled to open with me so I could get some paperwork done in peace, but with barely any sleep, I was running behind schedule.

Climbing behind the wheel of my truck, I drove towards town with the heat cranked. Fall was practically nonexistent this year as summer jumped right into winter temperatures. The first snow would be here before we knew it.

Hopefully that woman got new tires before the snow came. Even in the dark, I could see there was little to no tread on the rubber. I didn't miss her Colorado plates either, which meant she at least wasn't a stranger to icy roads.

Jacey's SUV was sitting in the parking lot by the time I pulled in fifteen minutes later. Parking my truck in its usual spot in the corner of the lot, I hopped out and headed inside the already unlocked front door.

Jacey had started working at Tumbleweed Feed around the same time I had. Fast forward eight years, I was now the owner of the store. Jacey was three years younger than me, just shy of turning thirty. With our work history, we got along great, and I considered her a friend, but nothing else.

I had no interest in dating right now. My mind was more focused on the store and Bottom of the Buckle Horse Rescue. My parents had started the rescue a few years before they had me, and even as our family grew, they never slowed down with the nonprofit. They lived and breathed BOTB, and all of my siblings supported it in their own way.

I was constantly trying to find potential homes for some of the rescues. With the foot traffic at the feed store, it was easy to strike up conversations with customers in an attempt to get them interested in adopting or volunteering.

"Good morning," Jacey greeted me as I walked by her on the way to my office.

"Morning," I grumbled.

She halted her sweeping, leaning up against the handle. "What's got you in a mood?"

"Don't know what you're talking about." I headed into my office, setting my travel mug and keys down on the desk.

Jacey's curvy form appeared in the doorway. "I'm not buying that."

Taking a seat in the chair, I blew out a long breath. "Don't know what to tell you."

"Please," she scoffed. "I know you, Len. Spill."

I met her gaze, noticing her hair. "Ponytail?"

She frowned. "The rain makes my hair frizzy. Stop avoiding the question."

Accepting that she wasn't going to back down, I sat back in my chair. "I got in an accident last night."

Her eyes widened. "A car accident? Are you okay?"

I leaned forward in my chair, setting my elbows on my knees. My body felt restless. "I'm fine. Just got rear-ended."

"The square body was hit? Is the truck okay?" She sounded more worried about the vehicle than she was about me.

My eyes narrowed. "You're asking if my truck is okay?"

"That thing is basically an artifact. You should be preserving it."

A frown pulled at my mouth. "It's a '78."

"Your point? You forget that's already forty-six years ago. The truck is only fourteen years older than you," she poked.

"You trying to say I'm old?"

She held her hands up in mock surrender. "You said it, not me."

Shaking my head, I shuffled through the papers on my desk, coming across the application for the interview today.

Jacey must have seen the stress on my face because she leaned her broom against the door frame and came to sit in the chair across from me. "Talk to me, Len."

"I'm just nervous about this interview."

"Isn't it supposed to be the potential employee who's nervous?"

I shot her another frown, then sat back in my chair again. "I need this one to work out. While I love the store-"

"And working with me," she added.

"I'm overworked," I continued, ignoring her comment. "I've barely had time to see my family lately. All these hours covering the register, on top of all the paperwork I have to do, I'm stretched thin."

Jacey scooted her chair forward an inch, resting her hands on my desk. "I know. You're doing everything you can. Don't pile the world on your shoulders."

"I have no choice. Not until I find someone to hire." Jacey hadn't wanted the manager position when the opportunity came up. I'd jumped at the opening, dying to dive further into the business side of things. Little did I know, I'd just be doing both jobs with a hundred more things on my to-do list.

Tumbleweed Feed was a mom-and-pop shop, created and owned by one of the locals before he retired, which was when I took over the business.

"I have a good feeling about this one," she said confidently.

"Let's hope."

I grabbed the register till from the safe under my desk and stood, walking out to the floor. Jacey followed, the broom back in her hands. Popping open the register, I set the till inside and closed the drawer.

Jacey got to work with the rest of the opening checklist, flipping the sign on the door from closed to open and turning on the rest of the lights in the store. I decided to stay up front with Jacey while I waited for the interview time to roll around.

A few locals came in, purchasing grain, chicken feed, horse dewormer, dog treats, you name it. For a small town, we filled a large demand and had a good amount of customers come through every day, which meant there was rarely a dull moment. We knew a lot of the customers by name, but every now and then, a stranger would come in, just passing through town. Not many people moved here, but when we did get the occasional new resident, we welcomed them with open arms.

"How's it going, Len?" Eric, one of the local cattle ranchers, asked as he set his bag of electrolytes on the counter.

I turned from the bulletin board beside the register. "Same old, same old. How's that rescue horse treating your daughter?" Eric's daughter had fallen in love with one of the mustangs that Bottom of the Buckle had taken in from an elderly lady who couldn't handle him.

He pulled his wallet out as Jacey scanned the barcode on the bag. "He's a wild one, but she's breakin' him in. Almost thought about callin' Brandy out a time or two."

My little sister's best friend, Brandy, broke horses on the ranch, and helped with the more unruly ones at the rescue. If anyone needed help with a green horse, they called her.

"She'd set him straight for sure. Some of 'em just take time, is all."

The bell on the door dinged as Jacey shut the register. She looked up to greet the customer that walked through the door, but I froze in place as my eyes landed on the woman, unable to believe who stood in the front of the store.

"That the new girl?" Jacey asked, noticing my body going ramrod straight.

"No. It's the woman who hit my truck."

3

OAKLEY

My hands moved to unzip my jacket, but they froze when I looked up to find hazel eyes staring at me.

You have to be kidding me. This guy again?

Forcing my fingers to work, I pulled on the zipper. The heater blasting inside the store erased any thoughts of the morning chill I'd been cursing not even seconds ago.

Closing the distance to the register, I focused my attention on the employee behind the counter rather than the six-foot-something man towering over me to my right.

"Is your manager here?" I asked her.

The woman - Jacey, according to her name tag - looked over to the man beside me, back to me, then at him again. "She *is* the new girl," she said to him.

"Excuse me?" I asked.

"You're Oakley Rae?" the man asked.

Pursing my lips, I angled my head to look up at him. "Yes?"

He heaved a sigh, his chest rising and falling with the action. Not that I was looking. Okay, I was.

"I'm Lennon. I own the store."

It took all I had in me not to let my jaw drop to the floor. Of course, the man who was my potential new manager was the same man who owned the truck I'd slammed my car into not even twelve hours ago.

I debated walking right back out the front doors, forgetting about the job altogether, but I needed it. I was quickly running out of funds, and there was no way in hell I was driving my ass back to Denver.

Maybe he didn't recognize me. It was dark, after all.

Reaching out my hand, I pasted on the best smile I could. "Nice to meet you, Lennon."

His brows pulled together. "We've already met."

Shit. He *did* recognize me.

Now this was even more awkward, if that was even possible.

"Right." I dropped my hand back to my side, taking the hint that he wasn't going to shake it. "I'm here for my interview in five minutes. I can wait if you're busy."

He looked around, then at Jacey. "You've got up front?"

She nodded, a mischievous smile pulling at her lips. "Good luck with the interview," she said to the both of us.

Lennon gave her a scolding look and walked around me toward the back of the store. His strides were longer than mine, so I had to quicken my pace to keep up with him.

He glanced back, seemingly noticing it, and slowed his pace a little. We walked down a short hallway and he opened a door, gesturing for me to go in first.

"Have a seat," he said as he came around the other side of his desk.

He pulled out his own chair as I sat in the one across from him. He sifted through the paperwork on his desk after he sat down, then leaned back in his chair, hands folded together.

"So, Oakley, why should I hire you?"

Uh, other than the fact that I'm going broke and surviving solely off boiled noodles and broth at the moment? "I'm a hard worker, a great multi-tasker, and never call out of work." I recited the list like it was ingrained into my brain. What else did employers want to hear other than that?

"Your resume was pretty bare when it came to job history," he pointed out.

I inwardly cringed. My parents had supported me, but I was anything but spoiled. Since getting out of college, I'd worked at my dad's firm filing paperwork for him. I didn't want to put that on my resume, though, because knowing my luck, my new employer would call his company asking about my experience and then he'd find out where I was. Without that in my history, finding a job at twenty-four was more difficult than you'd think.

"I know. But I'm a quick learner and I'm great with customers."

So was half the population.

He leaned forward, grabbing a pen to write something on the paper in front of him. My palms began to sweat as I watched the pen move. From where I was sitting, I couldn't make out the words, but I had no idea what he could possibly be writing from the little information I'd given him.

"You just moved here?" he asked.

"Yep."

He stared at me like he expected me to say more. After a few moments of silence, he asked, "From where?"

"Denver."

His chin tipped slightly. "Ah."

"What?"

He set the pen he'd been twisting in his fingers down. "Nothing."

Did he have something against Denver?

"Well, Oakley, I'm out of options here." That statement didn't make me feel good at all. "We haven't been getting as many people applying as I'd like to see, so you're hired."

I shook my head, thinking I heard him wrong. "I'm hired?"

He nodded.

"But I hit your truck."

His eyes froze on me from under the bill of his cap. "Being a good driver isn't a part of the job requirements."

Smart-ass.

"I'm really sor-"

He cut me off. "Don't apologize again. Please."

His eyes never left mine as I stood from the chair, holding my hand out above his desk to shake his. Dropping the car accident, I said, "Thank you, Lennon. I won't disappoint you."

He didn't so much as glance at my hand. "Come in tomorrow and we'll get started with onboarding."

Pursing my lips, I felt flames lick at my cheeks as I dropped my hand. I guess he wasn't a hand-shaking kind of guy.

I nodded once and turned on my heel to head out of his office. It went a lot better than I thought it would, especially given I'd rear-ended him last night. No matter how much he didn't want me to be sorry for the incident, I couldn't help it.

Out of all the people to rear-end, it had to be my future boss.

Starting over was already off to a terrible start, but I wouldn't let this stop me from creating a new life for myself.

4

LENNON

Six p.m. couldn't have come sooner. I needed a beer, or two. Oakley's white blouse tucked into her light wash skinny jeans with her sneakers clouded my mind. Her amber hair popped against her white shirt, and it was so damn long. I could imagine my fist wrapped around it, those green eyes boring up at me.

Fuck, seriously?

She was going to be my fucking employee. I couldn't be thinking of her like this. Especially not as her boss. She deserved my respect, not me fantasizing about her bent over my desk.

Shaking the thoughts from my head, I finished my third recount of the money in the till, locked it away in the safe, and grabbed my keys off the desk. Heading out of my office, I found Jacey in the canned dog food aisle facing the labels forward.

"Ready?" I asked.

"Yep."

We walked side by side out of the store, and I turned, locking the door behind me. My number one rule with my employees was that no one closed up alone. It wasn't hard when Jacey, Leo, and I were the only ones who worked here at the moment. Leo had started working here a few years ago as a cashier, but now he did a little bit of everything.

Though Bell Buckle was a small town where bad things rarely happened, it wasn't impossible. I'd rather my employees be safe than sorry.

"Is Oakley coming in tomorrow?" Jacey asked.

My steps faltered at the mention of her name and I hoped Jacey hadn't noticed. "Yeah, I was hoping you could show her how to use the register."

"Works for me."

I caught the devious smile on her face. "What?"

"Oh, nothing."

"Spill, Jace."

We approached her vehicle, which was a few spots over from mine. She turned with her back to her door. "She's cute."

"So?"

She shrugged. "That's all." I rolled my eyes as she turned to open the driver door. "See you tomorrow, Len."

I grumbled a goodbye and crossed the short distance to my truck, getting behind the wheel. I waited until Jacey drove away, then started my engine.

Driving out of the parking lot, I headed in the direction of my parents' ranch. I needed that cold beer and a distraction, and there wasn't a better way to get my mind off things than spending time with my dysfunctional family.

***

I parked my truck in the driveway next to my brother Callan's. The sun had already set, pushing the point that winter was already here with its late sunrises and early sunsets. Hopping out, I found my family on the back patio, sitting around a table that could practically seat half the town.

My mom thought it was necessary to find a table big enough for all of her kids, plus friends and significant others. Once one of us started having kids, I'm sure she'd find an outdoor set that could seat thirty instead of just twelve.

"Hey," I greeted everyone.

I bent to give my mom a kiss on the cheek before pulling a seat out next to her.

"How was your day, sweetie?" my mom asked.

My dad sat next to her with a cigar in his hand, his lips turned down with the typical frown he wore. I was starting to think the graying mustache just gave him the natural facial expression.

"As good as it can get," I replied.

Lettie, my youngest sibling, sat forward in her chair. Bailey, her fiancé, was next to her with his hand on her thigh. "Didn't you have that interview today?" she asked.

"Yep."

Callan took a bite of the barbeque chicken on his plate and waved his fork at me. "I think she's asking how it went, Len."

Everyone else's plates were cleared, indicating he had a riding lesson that went late. We all had dinner at my parents' house a few times a month. Beckham, our other brother, was rarely here, being busy on the road with bronc riding in the rodeo. We all hoped he'd retire soon, being three years away from thirty now.

"It went fine," I said.

"Mr. Talkative today, huh?" Bailey pressed.

"And you guys thought I was the closed-off grump." Reed scoffed. He was the closest in age to me, but we weren't as close as me and some of my other siblings. To be fair, though, Reed wasn't close with many people besides Bailey. We all grew up together, but Reed and Bailey were always hanging out together before Bailey and Lettie finally got together.

I looked to my mom for help, but she just offered me a small smile.

"I hired her," I announced.

Lettie let out a squeal. "That's so great! She seemed really sweet. I'm sure she'll do well at the store." Lettie was the reason Oakley had an interview set up in the first place. They'd met at a fundraising event for the horse rescue, and Lettie had suggested she apply to the feed store when Oakley asked if they were hiring.

I grunted, crossing my arms. "I don't know about sweet."

My mom gasped. "Lennon Bronson, you be nice when you're talking about her."

It wasn't that I didn't think she was nice. She was. In fact, she was so damn pleasant and delightful that I had to kick myself in the shin for wanting to spend more time around her.

"She's just an employee. I'm sure she'll quit in a few months and I'll be back on the hunt for another cashier."

Callan raised his fork again. "And *that* is why I will never work retail. Too many unreliable workers."

"Cal, you literally teach kids how to ride horses. You've had more no-shows this month than days I've had a sore back," Reed said. Being a farrier came with daily back pain, the job always having him bent over beside horses as he nailed shoes into their hooves.

Callan scowled at him. "That's definitely false. But I'm building a better clientele, in case you were wondering."

"More hot moms?" Bailey asked, a shit-eating grin on his face.

Lettie whacked him on the arm and I couldn't help the chuckle that passed my lips. Bailey feigned hurt, rubbing at his bicep.

"You kids are more entertaining than the evening news," my dad grumbled.

Reed's eyes narrowed. "We're not kids."

"With the way you lot act? I wouldn't have guessed it." It was my mom's turn to bump my dad's arm. "What? Do you hear them?"

"They're having fun, Travis. Try it once in a while," she said.

"I do have fun," he retorted.

Reed gave one of his rare smiles. "When? Reading the newspaper?"

My dad's signature frown deepened at the corners. "Crosswords are entertaining."

My mom rolled her eyes, standing from her chair to stack the plates. "Let me get those, Mom. Sit down," I insisted.

She did, stacking her utensils on her plate. "Thank you, Len."

"Of course."

Callan stood to help grab the dirty dishes, following me inside the house with them. I got to work loading them into the dishwasher as he wiped the counters.

"You talk to the rental guy?" he asked.

"I sent him an email last week, but no response yet." I'd been thinking about purchasing the building that we leased for Tumbleweed Feed. Since I took over the business, I didn't see the point in wasting money leasing the building any longer. I didn't see myself doing anything other than owning that store and helping out on the ranch, so it was the last step before it was officially mine.

"Make sure you follow up. There's so much spam going around, I lose emails all the time."

"I will," I replied.

If I was going to mention the car accident to anyone, it'd be Callan, but I decided to keep quiet about it. With my luck, one of my other siblings would overhear and tell the whole family, then before you'd know it, half the town would know. I didn't want Oakley to undergo judgment for rear-ending someone, and since there was no damage to my truck, I didn't see why I'd ever bring it up.

Despite that being the case, the memory kept replaying in my mind. Raindrops rolling down her cheeks, her hair dripping, her bare arms wrapped around herself for warmth. I mean, seriously, who went out without a jacket in a storm?

She may just be my employee, but some deeper part of me was determined to know more. That voice in the back of my head was the reason I had to keep our relationship strictly professional. There was no telling what would happen if I let it take over.

5

OAKLEY

Grabbing my sherpa-lined denim jacket, I headed out the door into the freezing morning air. The first snow would be here before I knew it, and my car was not ready for icy roads. It could use a new set of tires, but it'd have to wait until after my first paycheck, as I only had enough money for groceries for another week.

The Subaru may be old, but it was the first vehicle I'd purchased on my own with my allowance. I had a newer vehicle, but I left it in Denver because my dad had given it to me. I didn't want to take anything of his and have him hold it over my head to guilt me into coming back.

Hopping in my car, I cranked the heater, rubbing my hands together for warmth. Once it was warmed up, I backed out of the driveway, heading toward my new job.

My rental was a small, one-bedroom cabin-like house. It was more like a cottage, if you asked me. I wasn't looking for luxury, so it'd do until I had enough money to find a better place.

When I'd left Denver, I'd stupidly transferred all of the money my dad had given me back to his account and then blocked him on the banking app. I didn't want him seeing where I was and coming here to try to convince me to come home.

I'd been avoiding him ever since he tried to manipulate and control me. It all started after he found out my mom cheated on him and he immediately resented the fact I still talked to her. He was trying to get me to cut her off and take his side on everything. While I felt bad about the situation, I still loved my mom. I always would. A daughter's love for her mother didn't just disappear overnight. At least, that was the case for me. But that didn't mean I agreed with what she did.

My dad was never like this growing up, but something in him changed when he found out about my mom's affair. He wanted everyone on his side and to feel bad for him; everyone to cater to his needs through this hard time. While I obviously felt bad for him and what he was feeling, he was going about it all wrong. I could never condone cheating, but treating your daughter like this was wrong.

It was taking a mental toll on me, and I couldn't take it any longer.

He pushed me away without even realizing it, and now I was on my own. He called multiple times a day, but I never answered. I didn't want to hear his pleading to come home or listen while he talked bad about my mother.

As if he could feel me thinking about him, my phone rang from the cup holder beside me.

Speak of the devil.

I let it ring through, not wanting to risk reaching over to decline the call. The last thing I needed right now was another accident.

A few minutes later, I pulled into the parking lot outside of Tumbleweed Feed.

When Lennon said I was hired, I was utterly shocked. I rear-ended the man's truck, and yet, he was still willing to take a chance on me working in his store. I was excited for my first day because that meant I was that much closer to my first paycheck.

I had to admit, I was also a bit too eager to see Lennon again. During my interview, I could see his short, ash brown hair under the rim of his ball cap and the light dusting of facial hair along his jawline. He looked like he should have three kids and a wife by now. I wondered if he did.

He looked older than I was at twenty-four. He had to at least be in his thirties. Which brought me back to the thought of him possibly not having a family of his own. There had to be a reason the man hadn't settled down yet. I hadn't seen a ring on his finger, but maybe he didn't wear it to work.

Shaking the thoughts of Lennon from my head, I got out of my car and walked toward the front door of the store. I had to keep a clear head if I wanted to remember all the training I'd get today.

Would he be training me? Or would it be the curly-haired woman, Jacey?

Once inside, I pulled off my coat as Jacey smiled at me from behind the register. "Good morning. Ready for today?"

I smiled back at her, my cold cheeks slowly warming with the heat in the store. "I sure hope so. I'd hate to get fired on my first day."

She laughed. "I'm Jacey, by the way." She pointed at her name tag. "If you couldn't read."

"It wasn't on my resume, but I can assure you that is one trait I do possess. Nice to meet you, Jacey."

Her eyes briefly glanced at the coat in my arms before coming back to my face. "Why don't you go set that in the break room and come back up here so we can get started?"

"Is that in the back?"

She nodded. "Yep, right past Lennon's office."

Even just the mention of his name and knowing he was in the building right now made me nervous. I'd seen a lot of attractive, older men around Denver that would shamelessly flirt with younger women in the bars, but something about Lennon made me buzz with awareness.

He hadn't even tried flirting with me. He was just plain nice, aside from refusing to shake my hand. He had the whole broody, middle-aged thing down. Put that on top of his looks, and the way he'd acted after I hit his truck, and I was in trouble.

Striding through the store, I entered the hallway, finding that his office door was shut. I tried to shake the disappointment that came over me and passed his office, making my way into the break room and setting my coat on one of the hooks.

To make sure I had no distractions while I was training, I slid my phone into my jacket pocket and made my way back to Jacey at the front.

"The register is pretty easy," she started. "You just scan the items, the price automatically pops up, and if there's any deals, it'll adjust it itself. Once you've scanned everything, just hit this button." Her finger hovered over a key on the keyboard. "Then they'll pay, and the receipt will come out."

I nodded, my eyes scanning the register in case any questions popped up about what certain keys were, but they were all labeled and self-explanatory.

"If you ever have any troubles while using it, just come ask one of us. It can get finicky sometimes, but nothing we haven't dealt with before."

"Is there usually someone here with me?" I asked.

"Yep. Lennon schedules in twos, so no matter what shift you have, someone will be here with you. Len's one rule is that everyone walks out together, so just remember that at the end of each shift."

Of course, he had to be thoughtful, too.

"If there are no customers, you can face the shelves, dust, sweep, set out products. The usual when it comes to retail." She must not know I had basically zero job experience when it came to retail. "Lennon isn't too strict about keeping busy as long as the store looks nice."

"Face the shelves?" I asked, not sure what she meant.

"Make all the labels face forward, no crinkles in the bags. Basically just make it look neat and orderly," she explained.

"Sounds pretty easy, for the most part," I said.

She made her way around the counter to the bags of dog treats sitting on a shelf, working the wrinkles out of some of the bags so the labels were easier to read. "It is. It can just get a little stressful when it's busy, but other than that, it's pretty laid back. We don't typically get any grouchy customers either, which is nice."

I followed her, doing the same a few feet down the shelf. "I've heard some horror stories when it comes to old ladies and coupons."

She snorted. "That's exactly why Lennon doesn't mess with coupons. People get nasty with 'em."

The bell on the door dinged, and I turned to see a middle-aged man walking through the door.

"Morning, Jeff," Jacey greeted. With Jacey's use of his name, I assumed he must be a local.

"Good morning, ma'am. Who's this?" He eyed me, a grin wrinkling his face.

"Oakley. Can I help you with anything?" I asked.

Jeff chuckled, shaking his head as he fiddled with the button on the cuff of his denim jacket. "I've got this store memorized like the back of my hand. But thank you, miss."

I offered a smile, getting the feeling that ninety-eight percent of the customers who came in here would say the same.

He walked past me as I got back to work on the crinkles in the bags.

If this was how the rest of the day went, it wouldn't be too bad. But then again, the day had just begun.

6

LENNON

I glanced at my hands, which had been sorting through paperwork all morning. The callouses didn't disappear despite all of the desk work I'd been doing lately. All the time spent on the ranch kept them so hard that not a single paper cut pierced my skin.

If I wanted to purchase the building from the company that leased it out to Tumbleweed Feed, I needed to have my ducks in a row. There was enough money in the account for the down payment, so I wasn't worried about that. But I needed proof that we'd been paying monthly and on time, receipts of our expenses, and all the other boring shit.

I'd much rather be on the ranch than stuck in the dark, depressing office. I could go out on the floor for a bit, take a break from the paperwork, but then I'd have to see Oakley.

Every time her laugh echoed down the hall to my office, jealousy surged through me. Whoever the fucker was that got to hear her laugh and see her smile better know how damn lucky he was that I wasn't out there getting in between them.

I honestly had no right to be jealous, nor protective of her - she was just my employee after all - but I didn't want her fucking talking it up with the locals. I knew how sleazy some of these old men could be in this town, and I didn't want a single one of them laying an eye on her. If it was a hand, I'd cut it off. Simple.

Her resume being so bare raised questions in my head that I shouldn't want to ask. There were a lot of things I wanted to know about her. Like why she left Denver. And why she needed a job at a feed store in the middle of nowhere. Was there a reason she was in Bell Buckle? Family, maybe?

A phone went off from the break room next to my office. It was the same ringtone that'd been going off every fifteen minutes since Oakley walked back there and stowed her stuff away. I'd heard her soft footsteps on the linoleum and while I should have said good morning, or at least greeted her in some way, I'd stayed put in this chair, listening to her steps fade away back into the store.

Shaking my head, I stood up, deciding to leave the paperwork for later. I was going to go insane between the phone going off and thoughts of Oakley if I didn't go out there. It was time for my break anyway.

Opening the door to my office, I made my way to the front of the store to find Oakley at the register ringing Jeff up. Speaking of those old men...

"They always give me a ten percent discount," Jeff muttered to her, leaning too far over the counter, practically invading her space.

Her cheeks were as red as her hair, putting those little freckles on her nose on display. I approached her from the side, and she must've not seen me coming because she jumped when I said, "No one gets a discount."

Crossing my arms, I stood firm next to Oakley. Jeff wasn't going to pull one over on her. He straightened, holding his hands up, palms out. "I just had to give her the ol' ring-around. You got that, right, sweetheart?" He winked at her.

It took all I had in me not to reach across this counter, grab him by the neck of his shirt, and demand he apologize for calling her that.

She pursed her lips together as she pressed enter on the register's keyboard. "That'll be fifty-six dollars and twenty-seven cents, sir."

Good. She wasn't giving him the time of day.

He pulled the cash out of his wallet, setting it on the counter, then counted out the exact change. He added a quarter to the pile, and said, "That's for you."

A quarter. A fucking *quarter*.

Jeff had always been careless and a little too confident with the ladies, but I wouldn't let him get away with that shit. I grabbed the quarter, tossing it back at him, the coin clanging against the countertop.

"No tips, Jeff."

That was probably the worst thing I could have said, but I didn't want to scare Oakley by cutting the man's fingers off. If I'd voiced how pissed off I was, I couldn't guarantee that wouldn't happen.

God, when did I get so damn violent?

As the receipt was printing, I walked away, heading out of the store. I needed a coffee and something to eat or else I'd never get through the day.

And this was only day one of her working here.

Maybe she'd quit like all the others and things could go back to the way they were before she decided to slam her car into my truck's bumper and apply at the feed store. Couldn't she have chosen literally *any* other town besides Bell Buckle?

It was raining, but I'd forgotten my jacket back in my office and I was not about to go back in there just to get it. Then I'd have to walk by Oakley, and as much as I wanted to, I also wanted to stay as far away from her as possible.

Women who randomly showed up in small towns? They were nothing but trouble.

After half-jogging to Bell Buckle Brews, I shook the water off my baseball cap before walking inside.

"Good morning, Lennon," Sage greeted from behind the counter.

"Morning, Sage. Can I get a black coffee and a..." I trailed off, squinting my eyes to read the board.

"Jacey's usual?" she asked.

"No, uh... What do women usually order?"

A smile pulled at the corners of her mouth. "Seeing someone?"

My eyes shot to her. "No."

"Alright, alright. I won't pry. A vanilla latte is always a safe choice."

Vanilla sounded like something Oakley might like. "A vanilla latte, then. And two breakfast sandwiches, please."

She turned and grabbed a few things from the mini fridge, setting them up on the counter. "I'll have them up in a few minutes."

"Thanks." I took a seat at one of the tables, watching the rain as it trickled down the windows. It might as well have already been snowing with how cold it was out there.

Between the frigid temperatures already setting in and having to navigate the feed store with Oakley there, this was going to be a long winter.

7

OAKLEY

I grabbed the price sheet off the counter that Jacey had given me to work on in between customers. She was unloading bags off the pallets in the back, so for now, I was the only one up front.

Lennon had practically run out of the store after tossing the quarter back at Jeff. I wasn't going to accept it anyway, even though a quarter could really help me right now. Any spare change would come as a blessing until I got my first paycheck.

I didn't want to ask for it early and give off the impression that I was struggling. The last thing I wanted Lennon or Jacey thinking was that I'd steal from the register. The thought never even crossed my mind. I didn't have the heart to steal, and I really needed to keep this job if I wanted to eat anything other than salty, overcooked noodles.

The bell on the door dinged and I looked up, ready to greet the customer, but stopped short when I saw it was Lennon. He had two coffees in his hands and a paper bag held in the crook of his arm.

Assuming the second coffee was for Jacey, I went back to peeling at the sticker on the shelf. My stomach growled at the thought of coffee and a sandwich. I couldn't afford even granola bars right now, so I skipped on breakfast. I'd have to wait for my Cup of Noodles for lunch.

Lennon came up beside me, leaving a foot of space in between us. He held one of the coffees out to me, and I glanced at the cup before looking up at him.

"Here," he said. Rain that clung to his hat dripped down the sides, landing on his shoulders, soaking into the material of his shirt like the rest of the raindrops had outside.

I eyed the coffee, then looked back at him in question.

"I got you a coffee," he supplied, seeing the confusion written on my face.

I didn't want to seem too eager, gathering all my strength not to grab the cup and chug the delicious, nutty liquid, so I asked, "What kind?"

"Vanilla latte."

It was a common drink, but it was my favorite.

I slowly grabbed the hot cup from him, our fingertips brushing as he removed his hand. "Thank you," I said as my cheeks heated.

I hated how easy it was to turn my cheeks a million shades of red.

"You're welcome. I got you a breakfast sandwich, too. Just egg, sausage, and cheese." He held the brown bag up in his hand.

He got me food?

"I can't accept that, Lennon. The coffee is enough. I'm sure Jacey would love it, though." My stomach protested, letting out another long growl.

He arched a brow, his gaze moving to my stomach. My breath caught in my lungs. The man was looking at my body like I was the breakfast sandwich and he was the starving, broke girl who ran from her family.

"I think your stomach says otherwise."

I pursed my lips, my cheeks practically on fire at this point. "Can you put it in the fridge in the break room? I'll eat it on my break."

He nodded. "Of course."

I took a sip of the coffee, unable to wait any longer, and practically moaned when the warm liquid hit my tongue. God, I loved lattes. And with the cold, rainy weather? It made the coffee that much more mouthwatering.

Lennon didn't move to walk away. He just stood there, watching me as I sipped the drink.

"What?" I asked, lowering the cup.

"I, uh… I wanted to apologize for earlier." He moved his hand like he was going to scratch the back of his neck, but must've forgotten he had a bag of food in his grip because it hit his shoulder, and he dropped his hand back down.

"No need to apologize," I said.

"I was being cold to you, and it was uncalled for."

I pasted on a small smile. "I didn't even notice."

His eyes moved to my mouth and his lips tightened. "Well, regardless, I'm sorry for the way I acted."

I set my coffee on the shelf beside me. "Thank you for apologizing, but it really isn't necessary." I turned to continue peeling at the sticker, but paused, looking back up at him. "Why'd you give him the quarter back?"

His brows pulled together as he studied my face. "You're worth a lot more than twenty-five cents, Oakley. Don't let asshole old men think you're less than that."

Little did he know, twenty-five cents was about all I had to my name right now.

I didn't know what to say to that, so I turned my attention back to the sticker, hoping he'd take the message and walk away.

"You can have your phone on the floor with you, by the way."

My fingers stilled and I brought my gaze back to him. "What?"

"Your phone. I heard it ringing in the break room. You don't have to keep it in there."

"I don't want it on me, but thanks for letting me know."

He nodded, looking like he had something else he wanted to say, but instead of speaking, he walked past me toward his office.

Thank God. I felt like I couldn't breathe around him.

The way the water was dripping off his baseball cap and the thought of him thinking about me at the coffee shop enough to buy me a latte *and* a sandwich did things to my head that I didn't want to admit.

Jacey came out from the back with a dolly loaded with bags of feed. "You doing okay up here?"

"Yep, all good."

I was anything but.

***

After finishing the price changes and ringing up a few customers, Jacey relieved me for my break. I headed for the break room with what was left of my latte, my mouth watering at the thought of the breakfast sandwich in the fridge.

After days of cheap noodles, I was practically a dog looking at a steak after only having eaten kibble his whole life.

I passed the open door to Lennon's office, seeing him sitting at his desk out of the corner of my eye. His ball cap was low on his head as he studied something on the computer screen in front of him. He looked like he should be out in the elements on some ranch, not behind that desk.

He didn't glance up as I passed, but I didn't care. All I could think about was that sandwich. My stomach growled again as if it knew what was coming. Opening the fridge, I grabbed the brown bag, pulling the sandwich out. I didn't even care to heat it up, I just dug right in.

It tasted almost as good as the latte did, but nothing was better than coffee. I moved over to my coat as I chewed, pulling my phone out of the pocket of my jacket.

Eighteen missed calls.

My dad called a lot, but this was excessive.

Worried that something was wrong, I clicked his contact, dialing him.

He answered on the third ring. "Oakley?"

"Hey."

He sighed into the phone. "Where are you? Are you okay? I've been worried."

"I'm fine," I said. I wasn't going to give him any more than that in case he somehow figured out where I was and decided to come to Bell Buckle himself to bring me home. "Is there something you need to tell me?"

"Well, no, I-"

"Okay, then stop calling me."

The line was silent for a few seconds, then he said, "But, honey, I-"

"No," I interrupted again, "I don't want to talk to you right now. I need my space, okay? Can you please just respect that?"

"Can you at least tell me where you are so I know you're safe?"

"I'm safe. But unless there's some kind of emergency, I need you to give me a break."

The silence was back, and I debated hanging up the phone. I'd said all I needed to say.

"Okay," he whispered.

"Thank you." I hung up the phone, shoving it back into the pocket of my jacket.

I looked at my half-eaten sandwich, my appetite suddenly gone. Tossing it in the trash, I washed my hands in the sink and made my way back out to the floor.

I doubted my dad would give me the space I needed right now, but how else was I supposed to process the fact that my parents were split up, my mom cheated, and my dad wanted me to choose sides?

That was a choice no person should ever have to face. Yet here I was, finding myself right in the middle of it.

8

Lennon

My office chair squeaked as I leaned back, the sound interrupting the blissful silence of getting here before Leo and Oakley. I'd gotten a better night's sleep last night despite Oakley's words floating around in my head.

I'd overheard her on the phone in the break room from my office. I should have closed my office door, or at least not eavesdropped, but she sounded angry. Sweet, little Oakley had a flame to her, and fuck me for wanting to see it burn brighter.

Her conversation didn't sound pleasant and whoever she was on the phone with, she clearly didn't want to speak to them. I'd been curious who was calling her repeatedly all day. Her phone hadn't stopped ringing. But now I realized it had to be a boyfriend. Who else would she be telling to leave her alone?

Was that why she moved to Bell Buckle, to run from an ex?

My blood boiled at the thought of her feeling like she was in danger enough to the point she had to run. Was he abusive? Obsessive? *Clearly.* My pen cracked in my grip, and I loosened my hold. It was none of my business who she was on the phone with, but if I had to be on the lookout for a crazy ex trying to find her, I needed to know.

What if he came to the store looking for her and Jacey or Leo confirmed her employment here? It was a risk I wasn't willing to take.

As if the universe heard me thinking about her, the bell on the door dinged from the front of the shop, echoing back to my office. Soft footsteps padded on the linoleum until they came to the hallway and slowed.

"In here," I called out.

Oakley appeared in the doorway, fiddling her fingers together in front of her. Her denim jacket was stained with rain on her shoulders, and she was wearing the same light wash jeans, but instead of the white t-shirt she wore yesterday, she'd opted for the Tumbleweed Feed burgundy shirt with our logo on it - a tumbleweed rolling by a cow.

It was pretty corny, if you asked me, but Jacey helped design it, so it stuck.

"Good morning," Oakley said with a voice too small for my liking.

"Morning. I have your employee ID, so you can clock in and out, and your name tag. I'll show you how to use the punch system in the break room." I stood from my chair, coming around my desk to approach her. She stayed put, staring up at me as I got closer. I held out a hand, gesturing for her to head to the break room.

Snapping out of whatever trance she was in, she turned on the heel of her sneaker, passing through the break room door. I led her over to the tiny screen mounted on the wall.

"This is your ID." I handed her the Post-It note I'd scribbled it down on. "You just punch it in here, and whether you're clocking in or out, you choose the appropriate option after you punch in your number. You don't have to clock in or out for lunches and breaks. They're all paid."

She nodded, glancing down at the sticky note and punching the numbers into the screen. Once she was successfully clocked in, I shoved my hands in the pockets of my jeans, facing her.

"So why'd you move to Bell Buckle?" I asked.

She looked down at the small paper, folding it in fourths before shoving it in the pocket of her jacket. Her gaze moved up to me as she craned her neck back. "Just wanted a fresh start, I guess."

"You guess?"

She nodded, and I assumed that was all I was going to get out of her with that.

"How long have you been here?"

"A week or so. Have you lived here your whole life?"

I leaned a shoulder against the wall, keeping my eyes on her as she fiddled with the paper in her coat pocket.

"Yep. Born and raised here, and don't plan on leaving. Did you grow up in Colorado?"

She finally broke eye contact, looking around the room. "Yeah. I've never really been outside of Denver before coming here."

My eyebrows raised. "Really? Why choose Bell Buckle?"

A smile ghosted her lips as her eyes met mine again. "Would you believe me if I told you I was trying to find a Taco Bell?"

I laughed, unable to hold it in. That had to be the weirdest reason anyone ended up in this town. There wasn't even a Taco Bell within fifty miles of here. "This sure isn't no Taco Bell. Sorry to disappoint you, Oak."

Oak?

"It sure isn't, but that's okay. Bell Buckle's a cute little town. I quite like it."

My eyebrows rose again. "Really?"

"Yeah," she said hesitantly. "Is that wrong?"

"No, I'm just surprised. Not many people love small towns with nothing to do and no cities around."

She let out a small scoff. "Trust me, getting away from the city was a blessing. I'll take this town for what it is. Can I ask how long you've owned the store?"

"Yeah. About four years. I've worked here for eight, though."

"Oh, wow. That's a long time to work in one place."

I chuckled. "Yeah, but I don't mind it. I help out on my parents' ranch here and there, so it helps even out the fact that I'm stuck inside for most of my work day."

Her green eyes shone with something like longing as she asked, "Your parents have a ranch?"

"Yep. Grew up on it."

"So you have like, a horse or something?"

I smiled at the way she phrased the question. "Yeah. I've got a horse or something."

Her cheeks flushed and she looked down as a smile pulled at the corners of her mouth.

"Oakley, if there's some guy we need to be concerned about coming in here looking for you, I'd like to know."

Her head snapped up. "What?"

"I heard you on the phone yesterday in here. I didn't mean to eavesdrop."

"Why?"

My brows pulled together in confusion. "Because eavesdropping is invading your privacy...?"

She shook her head. "No, why do you care if there's some guy?"

"Because if that asshole walks into my store trying to find you, I'll gladly throw his ass out to the curb." I said it matter-of-factly. There was no other answer. No woman in my store was going to be disrespected and put in harm's way.

She was silent for a moment, gnawing on her lip as she focused on the screen on the wall. "It's not an ex," she said, not meeting my eyes. "I promise no one will come in here causing any problems. I'm sorry you thought-"

"You're apologizing?" I cut her off. No way in hell was she going to apologize for my concern for her wellbeing.

"Well, yes-"

"Don't apologize about your personal life, Oakley. Shit happens to a lot of people and they can't help it. It's not your fault. I should be the one saying sorry, I shouldn't have pried."

Her eyes finally found mine again. "It's okay. But nothing will come of it, I can at least assure you that."

Before I could reply, Leo walked into the break room. I glanced at the clock on the wall. The store opened in five minutes, and I still had to count the till and put it in the register.

"Oakley, this is Leo," I introduced him. "Leo, this is Oakley, our new hire."

Leo held a hand out, and she reached for it, the two of them shaking hands. My hands fisted as my eyes zeroed in on where their skin was touching.

I should've shaken her damn hand the other day.

"Store opens in five minutes. Make sure one of you is at the register," I grumbled before walking out of the break room and into my office.

My fingers punched the code into the safe and I grabbed the till with more force than necessary. It was going to be another long fucking day.

9

OAKLEY

Leo was nice. He was also checked out ninety-nine percent of the time, and while he was polite and engaged in small talk, I could tell he'd rather be anywhere else but here. I didn't blame him, though. I'd come to find that working retail wasn't exactly glorious and exciting.

He helped show me a few other things around the store, like the alarm we had to set before we left for the night, where they kept the cleaning supplies, and how to mark something down if it had a tear or hole in the bag.

The bell that hadn't stopped going off all morning dinged as two women walked through the door. I instantly recognized them from the booth at the Art & Wine event where they'd referred me to this job. I'd stopped by Bottom of the Buckle's booth at the festival my first day in town, looking for a job, when the shorter of the two had referred me to apply at Tumbleweed Feed.

"Hey, Oakley!" the woman with honey-colored hair greeted. I couldn't remember her name.

They ambled up to the register, smiles gleaming on their faces. "I'm so sorry, I don't remember your names."

"Lettie, and this is my best friend, Brandy," she said.

Brandy held out a hand. I hadn't spoken to her at the booth, so we hadn't talked before today. "Nice to officially meet you, Oakley. I've heard a lot about you the past couple days," she said with a wink.

I shook it, willing away the heat I felt creeping up my cheeks. I remembered Lennon was Lettie's brother, which made me nervous that he could have been talking to them about me. I hoped it was nothing but good things, but fear of hearing the worst kept me from asking.

"You should come with us to the bar tonight!" Lettie squealed.

"The bar?"

"Yeah, Outlaw's Watering Hole. I'm sure you need a night out."

"I'm not sure, I'm really busy-"

"You guys harassing my employee?" Lennon's deep voice interrupted.

My employee. There was nothing sweet about it, but it made my face turn as red as a tomato anyway.

Would I ever stop blushing when it came to Lennon?

"Oh, please. We're inviting her to hang out," Brandy said.

Lennon raised an eyebrow, crossing his arms. "Hang out, huh? With the two of you? She'll end up in jail on night one."

Lettie rolled her eyes. "Don't scare the poor girl." She faced me. "We're harmless, I swear."

Brandy shrugged. "Can't have fun without a little trouble."

Lennon frowned as I spoke up. "I'd love to."

Everyone's gazes turned to me.

"What?" Lennon asked at the same time Lettie said, "Yay!"

"Here's my number." Lettie grabbed a piece of paper off the counter, scribbling down the digits. "Do you want us to pick you up?"

"Sure. Do you want to pick me up after my shift?"

"I can drive her," Lennon offered.

I kept my gaze on the piece of paper with Lettie's number on it. "You don't have to do that. I'm sure Lettie is fine with picking me up here."

His gaze burned into the side of my face. "I'll already be here, so no point in making her go out of her way."

The way he said *making her go out of her way* made me feel like I was a burden. Regret at saying yes to them crept in, making me second-guess my decision to go. Maybe I should have just declined the offer to pick me up and driven myself.

Lettie looked between her brother and me. "That's fine with me. We'll meet you there, then?"

Moving my gaze up, I nodded. "We'll meet you there, I guess."

Brandy was smiling as Lettie squealed again, and they walked off into the store to get what they needed.

Lennon was still staring at me, but I refused to look his way. I folded the paper as many times as I could, shoving it in the pocket of my jeans before walking behind him and over to the shelves to face a few of the bags.

He unfortunately followed me. "I'm sorry if that came off wrong."

"It's fine," I clipped. I didn't know why I was upset over it, but I wanted to push it away and enjoy the rest of my day.

"If you want to go with them, you can."

My eyes finally met his, my head angling back to look up at him. "I don't mind going with you."

He looked like he was taken aback. "You don't?"

"No."

"Oh," was all he said.

"You're just my boss, Lennon. Nothing weird about getting a ride from you."

He nodded, his eyes narrowing a bit as he studied my face, likely looking for the truth in that statement. Hopefully he didn't look too hard because the only true part about what I said was that he was my boss.

I'd be alone with him in his truck. I wasn't sure how far Outlaw's Watering Hole was from here, but I hoped it was less than thirty seconds, because any longer alone with Lennon, I wasn't sure if I could control myself. I'd probably end up rambling about things he couldn't care less about and embarrass myself.

***

"How far is the bar?" I asked Lennon as he set the alarm to the store. The rain was coming down in buckets, so I pulled my hood on. My denim jacket did little to ward off the cold, but once I had enough money to spare, I'd buy a proper winter coat. For now, this would do.

"Couple blocks away," he answered as we walked across the parking lot. He hadn't put his hood on, but the water bounced off his hat as we hurried to his truck.

"Oh."

He glanced at me before pulling out his keys. "I'm not going to kidnap you, if that's what you're worried about."

My gaze shot to him. "What? No. I was just curious. Everything seems so close together here."

He came up on the passenger door, opening it for me. I slid in, wiping my hands on my jeans, though that did little to dry them as the material was wet, too.

He hesitated, watching the movement before his eyes found mine. "It's a small town."

"I know."

And we're off to a great start.

He closed the door, coming around the hood to get in on the driver's side. He started the truck as I buckled myself in, cranking the heater. "The first snow is going to be here soon," he pointed out.

I nodded, and turned to catch him staring at me.

"You should probably get some chains. Your tires looked pretty bald."

"You were looking at my car?" I asked.

"Well, I kind of had to when you hit me."

I looked ahead of me through the windshield, the rain sliding down the glass. "I guess you're right. I'm really sorry about that, by the way."

He shifted the truck in reverse, backing up a few feet before shifting into drive and heading out of the parking lot. "You don't need to keep apologizing for it, Oakley."

"I just feel bad, okay? Can a girl not apologize for ramming into the back of your truck?"

I had a lot of guilt on my conscience, and if apologizing for the hundredth time for rear-ending him made me feel better, I was going to do it.

A few minutes later, he pulled into a parking lot outside a big wooden building. The only thing indicating it was a bar was the giant orange neon sign out front. In the dim light from the overcast sky, the sign glowed bright, illuminating the mist around it.

Lennon killed the engine, turning to face me. "You may feel bad, but just know that I've let it go. It happened, and you're okay, and that's all that matters."

Our eyes were stuck in some trance as I saw something flit over his face. Like seeing the sun after a week's long storm. But it was gone in an instant, and then he was getting out of the truck, coming around to open my door for me.

"Thank you," I mumbled as I got out.

He nodded in response and closed the door. He'd parked close to the front door of the bar, so thankfully, on our way inside, we didn't get too soaked. I shrugged out of my jacket as we walked over to the table Brandy and Lettie were at by the pool tables. A few guys I didn't recognize were playing a game, not noticing us as we approached.

"You made it!" Lettie squealed.

She wrapped me in a quick hug, then released me. "I didn't know what you wanted to drink, but we can go get it together. I need a refill anyway."

Lennon draped his coat over the back of the chair beside me, and the guys at the table turned to find us standing there.

"Thought your ass was never going to show up," the guy with the beige cowboy hat said. He ambled over to us and shot me a smile, holding out his hand for me to shake it. "I'm Bailey. And I take it you're Oakley?"

Shaking his hand, I smiled. "Yep. I get the feeling you've heard about me, too?"

He dropped my hand, taking a swig from his beer he'd grabbed off the table. "Lettie here won't shut up about ya."

She glared at him. "Be nice."

So it wasn't Lennon who had talked about me. A small bit of disappointment crept in, but I willed it away. Tonight was meant to be fun, and being down in the dumps over something so miniscule wasn't helping.

The other two men ambled over, pool cues in hand. "Oakley, this is Reed and Callan, my brothers," Lennon introduced them.

"He'd introduce you to Beck, but he's too busy in the big leagues," one of the guys said. He had dirty blonde hair that curled at the nape of his neck under his baseball cap.

"Big leagues?" I asked.

Lennon looked down at me. "He does rodeo. Rides broncs for some dumb ass reason."

"Callan's just butthurt because he deals with teaching kids how to ride horses all day," the man with the black cowboy hat and tattoos joked. I guessed that one was Reed.

Callan picked up his beer, taking a long swig. "Better than breaking my back shoeing horses. Plus, I like kids. I don't see the problem with my job."

Lettie grabbed my arm, whispering in my ear, "If we don't go now, we'll be stuck listening to them argue about whose job is better."

I followed her lead to the bar with Brandy at my heels. Neon beer signs illuminated the dark atmosphere of the bar, and the smell of beer and whiskey filled the air. There were people dancing in the middle of the room, but it wasn't packed for a weekday.

"What can I get you ladies?" the bartender asked over the music playing.

"Three shots of tequila, and whatever else they want," Brandy said.

"I'll just have a mojito, thanks," I told the man, already calculating how much money I'd have left over after a drink.

"Me too!" Lettie shouted. She seemed to already be buzzed, or maybe she was just typically this hyper.

Brandy faced us with an elbow on the bar as he got to work with our order. "I've got a beer at the table, so I'm only doing the shot."

"You know it won't be the first." Lettie smiled, the act bordering on evil.

I wasn't huge on taking shots, so this would be torture. I preferred sweet drinks over the burning taste of straight alcohol.

"So, Oakley, do you have any siblings?" Brandy asked.

I shook my head. "Only child."

Lettie gaped at me. "God, you're lucky. Having four brothers is the absolute worst."

"They don't seem too bad," I said.

She rolled her eyes as Brandy said, "The lot of them aren't. But one in particular grinds my gears."

I raised one of my eyebrows. "Really? Which one is that?"

My eyes drifted back to the guys as she said, "Reed. He's an asshole. Stay as far away from him as possible if you can."

"The one with the tattoos?" I asked, to make sure I had the right guy. He didn't seem like an asshole at first glance.

Brandy inhaled deeply. "Please do *not* talk him up like that."

"Oh, please, Brandy." I brought my attention to Lettie as she spoke. "Reed's nice. He and Brandy just have some hate-thing going on," she not-so-quietly mumbled to me.

Brandy gaped at her. "*Hate-thing*?"

The bartender set the two drinks on the bar next to the shots he'd lined up as we spoke. "What would you call it?" Lettie asked.

"He's fucking Satan, Lettie! He had to have come from the depths of hell."

I laughed, grabbing for my drink. Brandy grabbed it from my hand, replacing it with a shot. "Nuh-uh. You're taking this first."

"Peer pressure much?" I joked.

"Ain't peer pressure if you're enjoying it. C'mon." She hit the bar with her shot once, then tipped it back, swallowing it in one gulp. Lettie repeated the movements, so I followed suit, cringing at the taste as it burned down my chest. My eyes pinched shut, my mouth pursing tight as I shook my head, trying to rid the taste from my tongue.

Grabbing my mojito, I sucked on the straw, turning my gaze to find Lennon watching me with his hands in the front pockets of his jeans, leaning back against the table with his feet crossed in front of him. Reed and Callan were talking a few feet away from him at the pool table, but he wasn't paying attention. All his focus was on me, and I was turning to cinders under his gaze. Chugging a gallon of tequila would burn less than what his eyes on me did.

10

Lennon

Callan, Reed, and Bailey faded into the background as all my attention was fixed on Oakley standing by the bar. She was still in her work uniform, but that didn't dull any of her beauty from where she stood.

Her face scrunched in the most adorable way when she knocked back the shot. It was clear she didn't do them often, which made it all the more cute.

Since when did I start fucking say shit like adorable and cute?

Her eyes had caught on mine from across the bar, and even in the dim light, I could see her cheeks flush a deep shade of crimson. I hated how much I enjoyed looking at her and seeing that damn smile. When those teeth flashed, it was like opening the curtains in the morning to let the sun shine in.

It felt like my life had a constant gray cloud hovering above me until Oakley rear-ended me. Up until that point, every day felt like the same, typical routine. But now I had something to look forward to - seeing her.

Even if she was just my employee.

After working at Tumbleweed Feed with the same two employees for as long as I could remember, it was nice having a new face to see around there.

That's what I was telling myself.

I'd forced myself to look away and join the guys with their game of pool. I was playing a round with Bailey when the girls finally came back over to us.

"Having fun?" Lettie asked, coming up to Bailey, who put his arm around her shoulders.

Reed had a stern expression on his face as he regarded Brandy, clearly seeing how inebriated she was. Her beer had gone warm on the table, seemingly forgotten about, but just a few shots would get her buzzed. We all knew she was a lightweight.

Brandy smirked. "What's with the face, Satan?"

"Satan?" Reed repeated.

Oakley leaned a hand on the back of a chair, her second mojito in the other. "She thinks you're Satan."

I looked down at her as her lips wrapped around the straw of her drink, her eyes peering up at me. Clearing my throat, I moved my gaze back to Reed and Brandy. That was not the image I needed in my head right now.

BEAT AROUND THE BUSH

Callan was bent over the pool table, taking a shot at one of the balls, ignoring the rest of us. I didn't blame him.

"Whatever makes you feel better," Reed grumbled, taking the next shot after Callan missed.

Brandy frowned. "I never feel good when I'm around you."

As she said it, Reed missed the ball with his cue, then immediately straightened and tossed the stick on the table. He walked around, grabbing his beer and stomping off to the bar.

"Grump," Brandy muttered.

"Anyone going to take over for him?" Callan asked as if he was oblivious to what just transpired.

Lettie raised her hand. "I will!"

Brandy and Bailey stood by cracking corny jokes as Lettie went up against Callan in a new round. Beside me, Oakley sucked on her straw again, the contents of the drink now gone, so it made a loud slurping noise. She set the glass on the table, pouting out her lower lip.

I turned to face her. "Do you want another?"

Her eyes shot up to me as if she'd forgotten I was standing there. "No. I should probably stop or I'll end up saying things I'll regret."

"Like what?" I asked, reaching up to pull off my hat and comb my fingers through my hair. I set it on backwards and her eyes widened. I didn't need the bill over my eyes in the bar. It was hard enough to see her in the neon lights.

"What?" I asked.

"Put it back."

My eyebrows drew together in confusion. "Put what back?"

She stood as still as a statue. "The hat."

"My hat?"

"Yes, your damn hat. You can't wear it like that."

"Why can't I wear it like this?"

She maneuvered around the chair, her hip bumping the back as she reached up to grab my hat, taking it off and setting it back on with the bill facing forward. "Much better."

I stared down at her as I asked, "Do I look bad with it backwards or something?"

"Quite the opposite." She must've realized what she said because she froze, her eyes widening.

"Did you just compliment me?"

She covered her mouth, letting out a muffled, "No."

"It sounds like you did."

Her hands dropped, her green eyes glowing in the lights. "Only with the hat."

"With it like this?" I gestured to the hat, then grabbed it, flipping it backwards. "Or like this?"

She shrieked, standing on her tiptoes to reach up and pull it off again. "No more hat. This is dangerous."

I raised an eyebrow. "Dangerous, huh? How so?"

She shoved the hat on her head, her red hair billowing out in waves around her shoulders. "It just is. So I'll be keeping this."

"I don't get it back?"

She shook her head, the bill casting a shadow over the top half of her face. "Not until you can control yourself with it."

I chuckled. "I think it's you who needs to be controlled."

Her mouth opened and closed, searching for words that she couldn't grasp. I didn't mean for what I said to come off as insinuating anything, but that's how she must've taken it.

Reed appeared next to me, leaning in. "I think we should get the girls home."

Satan saves the day. I wasn't sure how much longer I could stand this close to Oakley and keep myself contained. Contrary to her belief, I was controlling myself as best I could right now.

I turned to find Lettie and Brandy making a spectacle of themselves dancing with the pool cues, suggesting they were stripper poles. They never ceased to find fun in the smallest of things.

"Oakley came with me, so I'll take her home. You good with them?" I asked him.

Reed nodded. I wasn't sure if they drove in one vehicle or many, so I'd leave that part up to them. My main concern was getting Oakley home. The guys would take care of Lettie and Brandy. They always did.

"You ready to call it a night?" I asked Oakley, who was trying to act casual about using the chair behind her to steady herself. She looked so damn pretty wearing my hat. I was half convinced I should let her keep it forever and make it a part of the dress code at work.

"Hmm... I don't know."

"Now you want to drink more?"

She crossed her arms. "And if I do?"

I shrugged, a smile threatening to bloom at her stubborn behavior. "I guess I could carry you out of here."

She snapped straight, grabbing her jacket off the chair. "Maybe the hat isn't the only thing you need to control yourself with."

I reached around her, my fingers wrapping around the material of my jacket. My arm brushed hers as her eyes stayed locked on mine. I lowered my voice, leaning down to bring myself closer to her. "What else should I control myself with, Oakley?"

Her breathing picked up pace, her chest rising and falling with the action. Her eyes darted back and forth, searching mine. She wasn't going to reply, but I didn't care. I'd wait forever if it meant I got to stay this close to her. She smelled like vanilla and cinnamon, and I was getting fucking high.

A hand slapping against my back pulled me out of Oakley's orbit. "Get home safe," Bailey said as he passed, Lettie's hand in his.

"You, too."

I turned my attention back to Oakley, who was shrugging her denim jacket on. "We can go," she said.

"Are you sure? We can stay if you want to."

She wouldn't meet my gaze as she said, "It's okay. It's late anyway."

I nodded and she turned, heading for the door. I followed close behind, resisting the urge to place my hand on her back as we walked. As we approached the door, I came around her, opening it for her.

She gave a tight, closed-lip smile as she passed under my arm. As soon as we were outside, she started shivering. The cold was a shock to the warmth from the bar and the alcohol. "Do you want my coat?"

She spun around and I almost ran right into her. "Your coat?"

"You're shivering."

"It's your only coat." She reached up, pulling my hat off her head and holding it out to me. "I shouldn't have taken this."

I didn't move to grab my hat from her. I didn't even glance at it. I shrugged my jacket off, holding it out beside her outstretched hand. "A trade."

She finally brought her gaze up to mine, those green eyes shining brighter than any gemstone. "That's not how a trade works."

"It's not?"

"Well, they're both yours."

"I'm giving you my jacket in exchange for my hat. I'm pretty sure that's how a trade works."

She frowned up at me, her pink lips in a tight line. "Fine." She reached up on her tiptoes, setting my hat back on my head, *not* backwards, then grabbed my jacket, opening it up to slide her arms through the sleeves. It was big on her, but I liked her in my clothes. I'd also like her without any clothes.

Jesus Christ.

"Can we go now?" she asked.

I took the few steps to my truck, opening the passenger door wide for her. "After you."

She moved from her spot, sliding into the seat. Her hands were buried in the sleeves of my jacket as she crossed her arms.

"Gotta buckle in, Oak."

She sighed and reached for the seat belt, clicking it into place. Satisfied, I closed the door, coming around to the driver's side. I got in and started the truck, cranking the heater. It wasn't raining now, but it was freezing out as the night air settled in. Oakley's head lolled back against the seat as I drove out of the parking lot.

"Where do you live?" I asked her, hesitating before turning onto the main road so I knew which direction to go.

"Melody Drive," she mumbled.

I knew exactly where that was. Having lived in Bell Buckle my entire life, I knew every street and back road like the back of my hand. Melody Drive wasn't the nicest neighborhood. Lots of people who couldn't afford properties lived down there. Most of the houses were barely big enough for a family of three.

It was a short drive past a few hay fields before I turned onto her street.

"It's the one with the white mailbox," she said.

Keeping my eyes peeled, I drove until I found the one. I pulled into the driveway and killed the engine, getting out and coming around to open her door. By the time I had it open, she had her seat belt off, but didn't move to get out of the truck.

Her temple was leaning against the headrest as she looked at me. "You don't have to walk me to my door," she slurred.

"I at least want to make sure you get inside okay." I wasn't going to just drop her at the curb and leave.

She went to get out, then paused, eyeing me. "You're not going to try to sleep with me, are you?"

I chuckled, shaking my head. "No, Oakley. You're drunk."

She raised an eyebrow. "If I wasn't?"

"Well, you are, aren't you?"

She pulled her bottom lip in between her teeth like she was trying to decide if she truly was drunk or not. "Yeah, I guess I am."

She slid out of the seat, our bodies mere inches from each other as she got her bearings on her two feet. "Do you want your jacket back now?" she whispered.

A smile pulled at the corners of my mouth. "Why are you whispering?"

"I wasn't sure if you wanted people to hear."

"Oak, look around. There's no one here."

She did, pouting out her lower lip as her eyes met mine again. "Well, do you want your jacket back?" she whispered again.

I tried my best to hold back my laugh and shook my head. She was so fucking cute. "No. Come on, it's cold."

This time as we walked, my hand hovered near her shoulder blade. My palm itched to feel her tiny frame under my jacket, but I willed it to stay an inch away.

We approached her front door and she dug through her pockets under my jacket, searching for her keys. Once she found them, she tried to shove one in the keyhole, but failed miserably.

After many unsuccessful attempts, I finally grabbed them from her, inserting the key myself and twisting the lock.

"I'm sorry. It's cold and I probably drank too much and-"

"Oak, it's fine." I cut her off. I could listen to her ramble all day, but not if she was apologizing. She apologized too damn much, and I hated whoever instilled in her that she had to be sorry for such little things.

I pushed the door open and she walked inside, then turned, looking at the door frame like it was some barrier that would keep her safe from me. Maybe we needed to keep that barrier up, if only to prevent ourselves from the complications of this going further. She was buzzed, so I wouldn't do anything with her, but that wouldn't stop her from trying. Alcohol made people do things they may not want to do sober, and I didn't want things to be awkward at work.

"You can come in, if you'd like," she said.

And there goes that barrier.

My hand idly rubbed at the back of my neck as I stepped in, closing the door behind me. She flicked on a light, showcasing the small living room with a tiny kitchen attached. There was all the necessary furniture, but nothing really of hers, it seemed like. No pictures, no girly rugs. It looked like a seventy-year-old woman had thrifted all the furniture from a retirement home.

She plopped on the couch, looking over at me taking in the room. "Sorry it's so-"

I pinned her with a look. "Oak."

"Sorry."

I shook my head, closing the distance and taking a seat next to her. I kept a foot of space between us, not wanting to give her the impression I wanted to do anything more. My only desire right now was to make sure she got into bed and remembered to lock her front door.

I glanced over at her to find her looking down at her covered hands. "Why do you do that?"

"Apologize?"

"Yeah."

She pulled at the edge of her sleeve before answering, "I guess I'm just used to it."

I watched her, keeping silent as I waited for her to elaborate.

"My dad has this thing about perfectionism that put some pretty high expectations on me, so every little thing... I just apologize."

It made sense. If my parents had high standards for me, I'd probably get in the habit of doing the same, but that didn't mean it was right. She shouldn't apologize for being herself or having her own way of doing things.

Figuring she'd probably appreciate a subject change, I asked, "Do you have a heater in here?" It wasn't much warmer in here than it was outside and that didn't sit right with me.

She looked down at her fingers, picking at a spot on her thumb. "I do."

"Do you want me to turn it on?"

"I can't really afford the gas bill right now," she admitted quietly.

I leaned back against the couch, draping an arm over the back. "Do you need an advance in your paycheck?"

Her gaze shot to me. "No. You don't have to do that. I'll be fine until my first paycheck comes in."

I nodded, not believing that for a minute. She must have left Denver in a hurry, because it was obvious she had no money saved, and no plan in place when she ended up here.

She grabbed the wool pillow from beside her on the couch and laid her head on it, curling her legs up so they didn't touch me. I felt bad that she was laying on the couch. She should get some rest in her actual bed, not on the couch just because I was here. I watched her for a minute, appreciating the simplicity of this moment. I shouldn't want to take care of her but, fuck, I *wanted* to.

"Oak."

Her eyes were closed, giving no indication that she heard me.

"Oakley," I said.

Nothing.

I stood up and came over to kneel in front of her, my eyes landing on her slightly parted lips as her breathing deepened with sleep. The alcohol must have pulled her under quick. Feeling bad if I woke her, I gently slid my arms under her body, lifting her from the couch. She groaned as I cradled her to my chest, walking over to what I assumed was her bedroom door.

I nudged it open with my boot, not bothering with a light since the one in the living room illuminated the space enough to see where I was going. Bending down, I pulled back the comforter and laid her on the bed, pulling the blanket over her.

On instinct, she nuzzled into the pillow, her amber hair bright against the white pillowcase even in the dark. My hand reached up to brush the strands out of her face gently so I didn't wake her.

It wouldn't work out even if we did end up getting together somehow. I'd never get a lick of sleep with her laying next to me, not with my inability to stop staring at her. Despite my better judgment, I brushed my lips across her temple. Her skin was smooth, and I could smell the sweetness of whatever hair product she used. She was like honey in coffee, a sweetness against the bitterness.

Standing, I headed out of the room, closing her bedroom door with a silent click. I searched the walls for the thermostat. Once I found it, I pressed a few buttons, turning on the heat. It read that it was forty-nine degrees in here. That was too damn cold for me to be comfortable with. I couldn't leave her in this little house knowing she was cold. I'd pay the damn gas bill if I had to.

Crossing to the kitchen, I found a sticky note and pen in one of the drawers. I began writing, but thought better of what I wrote and scrapped it, crumpling it in a little ball and opening the trash can to throw it away. I paused, seeing that her trash was full of ramen noodle containers. My heart squeezed thinking this was all she was surviving off of right now.

I turned back to the paper and wrote a short message, leaving it in the middle of the counter so she'd see it, then pulled out my wallet, setting some cash on the counter.

I hoped she didn't take it the wrong way and used it to get a decent breakfast tomorrow. Sodium-filled noodles wouldn't give her any energy or vitamins or anything her body needed to thrive.

Before I could talk myself out of leaving, I headed for her front door, grabbing her keys on my way. I locked the door behind me and headed for my truck.

I wasn't sure what was going on in Oakley's life, but I was now determined to find out.

11

OAKLEY

My eyes squeezed shut as the water sprayed my face, doing little to wash away my headache. I'd been buzzed enough to lose my filter, but not enough to forget about last night. Images of Lennon with his hat backwards at the bar, taking his jacket off for me outside, and him standing in my living room flashed through my mind.

Lennon had been in my house.

Panic seized me as I practically punched the knob to turn the shower off, then grabbed a towel and burst out of my room. I took in the empty space, finally taking a breath. Thank God he hadn't spent the night.

My eyes caught on something sitting on my kitchen counter as I went to go back into my room, making me pause. Holding the towel closed around me, I walked over to the items, seeing there was a sticky note and cash laying there.

I read what he'd scribbled down, then rubbed my eyes, reading again:

For the heater and breakfast. Keep the coat. - L

"Keep the coat?" I said out loud. Was he mad at me? This was why I hated texting, you could never tell someone's tone of voice. I now learned that I hated notes, too.

Not bothering to count the cash, I pocketed the wad of bills. There was no way I'd be accepting his money. I'd give it back to him today, even though I wasn't scheduled to work. That didn't mean I couldn't go to the store and give it to him.

Maybe I could bring him a coffee, too. To thank him for driving me home last night. Of course, it'd be coming out of the money he gave me, but it wasn't essentially wrong, given it was his money, his coffee. I was just the errand runner at that point.

Heading for the thermostat, my finger punched the "off" button. The heater was nice after a cold night, but now I'd have to figure out how to pay the gas bill and be able to afford groceries, chains for my car, and most likely a new set of tires.

I couldn't be mad at him for turning the heater on. He probably felt guilty leaving me in a house that was almost the same freezing temperature as outside, and it wasn't his fault he didn't know the extent of my money situation right now.

This was only temporary. I'd be back up on my feet in no time.

No guy had ever been so sweet as to drive me home from the bar, walk me inside, and make sure I got into bed. I didn't remember anything past the couch, so he had to have carried me to the bed, unless I sleep-walked and tucked myself in on my own, which was extremely unlikely. I slept like the dead.

Speaking of him driving me home...

If my car wasn't here, I had no way of going to get it. I ran to the front window, looking out to see if my car was there.

I found it sitting in my driveway.

Did he bring it home for me?

He must've taken my keys and had one of his brothers help him drop it off. But why would he do that?

Ignoring his offer on the note to buy myself breakfast with the money, I opened the upper cabinet to pull out yet another cheap cup of ramen. I'd lost track of how many I'd consumed at this rate. I was surprised my body wasn't shutting down from the amount of sodium in these things.

Filling a pot with water, I set it on the tiny two-burner stove and turned the heat to high. They tasted a little bit better if I used the stove instead of the microwave. Or at least that's what I told myself.

While I waited for it to boil, my eyes scanned the note Lennon had left on my counter. My mind drifted back to him writing notes during our interview, wondering if whatever he'd scribbled down was positive or some time frame of how long he'd give me a shot for until he decided to fire me.

My phone rang from where I must have left it last night on the small table next to the couch. Walking over, I picked it up, seeing my mom was calling.

At least it wasn't my dad again.

To my surprise, he'd stopped calling after I'd asked him to. He was worried about me, but he was going about it the wrong way. My mom wasn't as overbearing as my dad, so I answered the call, setting the phone on speaker. I'd assure her I was fine, then bring Lennon his money back. Then I could come home, crawl under the blankets to ward off the already-cooling house, and nap all day.

"Hey, Mom," I answered.

"Oakley, your father told me you left home." Okay, maybe she *was* going to be as overbearing as my dad.

Setting the phone on the kitchen counter, I braced my hands against the cool ledge. "I couldn't stay in Denver."

"Honey, talk to me. What's going on?" Her accusing tone went soft, her concern seeping in and making me miss home.

Telling my mom that my dad was trying to make me pick sides between the two of them was the last thing I wanted on her mind. She knew how mad he was, but I didn't want to cause a bigger feud than there already was between them.

"I just felt like a fresh start would help clear my head. I'm safe, I promise. I've got a little house I'm renting and everything." Well, everything besides money in my bank account, a car ready for the snow, and food in my cabinets.

"Can I ask where this fresh start landed you?" I could hear the smile in her voice. She'd always been my biggest supporter, and I loved her for it. She'd always tell me that no idea was stupid, even if it fails. She was one of those live-life-to-the-fullest kind of women, and that meant no holding back.

Last I knew, my parents weren't on speaking terms, so there wasn't any harm in telling her. "Bell Buckle. It's a really small town in Idaho."

"Are there hot cowboys?" she asked jokingly.

I smiled, missing my mom all the more. "There may be."

"Well, when you rope one in, I want to hear all about it."

Shaking my head, I turned from the phone to turn the burner off on the stove, removing my now-boiling pot of water and pouring it into the styrofoam cup full of dried noodles.

My mom was living with her new boyfriend in Denver, but I felt awkward asking how they were doing. It felt like I was going behind my dad's back in some way if I talked about the new guy. Their relationship was rocky, but I never thought she was unhappy enough to find another man. The news had come as a shock, and while I didn't condone what she did, I was too close with my mom to hate her for it. She was like my best friend growing up, but her actions changed that dynamic. I did my best to keep things somewhat the same with her, but what she did to my dad was always in the back of my mind. "Can I call you later? I have a few errands to run since it's my day off."

Dumping the rest of the water down the sink, I set the pot back on the stove to cool down, then turned back to the phone.

"Sounds permanent if you have a job, too," my mom commented.

She was asking if I was staying, and honestly, I wasn't sure how to respond. I liked it here so far, but I wasn't sure if it was my final destination. I could go anywhere I wanted. Once I had the money, of course. Did I want to stay in Bell Buckle for the foreseeable future? Lay down roots and establish a life here?

"I'm not sure about Bell Buckle yet, but I'll let you know."

"Where are you working?" she asked.

"A feed store. It's pretty laid back and my coworkers are nice." I was careful to leave Lennon out of it. If my mom heard there was a sweet, walk-you-to-the-door, take-care-of-you-when-you're-drunk type of guy involved, she'd never get off the phone.

"Can't wait to hear all about it. Enjoy your day, sweetie. I love you."

"Love you, too. Bye, Mom." I hung up the phone and grabbed my noodles, ripping the lid the rest of the way off and throwing it in the trash. I saw there was a piece of paper crumpled on the top of my mountain of styrofoam cups in the trash. The same type of paper that Lennon had scribbled his note on.

I froze, wondering if he saw the contents of my trash. He must have thought *I* was trash for eating ramen for breakfast, lunch, and dinner.

I reached into the bin, grabbing the note off the top, and unfolded it, doing my best to flatten out the wrinkles.

There were a few scribbled out bits, but at the end - when he must've given up - it read:

It's too cold in here, so I turned the heater on. I'll cover the cost, just stay warm.

And I swore it said *for me* at the end of the sentence, but it was so blacked out with ink, I could barely make it out.

Tossing the paper back in the trash and grabbing my food off the counter, I headed for the couch and imagined it was a dish from a Michelin star restaurant.

***

I was cursing myself for not bringing a warmer jacket with me when I left Denver. I'd layered my gray sweatshirt under my denim jacket, but the cold still seeped through the fabric, biting at my skin. I refused to wear Lennon's jacket, no matter how cold it was. I appreciated the thought behind it, but wearing it was a one-time thing. I'd also spaced on my way out and completely forgot it at home.

"Good morning," I greeted the woman behind the counter of Bell Buckle Brews.

"Good morning," she said right as a child darted out from the door behind the bakery display. "Avery, please go draw while Mommy works. I'll be back there in an hour."

"But I don't wanna draw," the little girl complained as she tried to open the bakery case, her eyes locked on a pink donut.

I smiled at the girl as the woman turned her attention back to me. "Sorry about her. I don't have a babysitter at the moment, so she has to come to work with me."

"Don't be sorry, it's totally fine. I love kids," I said. "How old is she?"

"I'm five, but my birthday is soon so I'm almost six," Avery answered for her mom.

"Are you having a birthday party?" I asked her.

Avery nodded, smiling wide. "It's gonna have a lot of pink stuff. Mom said I can pick out the colors for my cake."

"In a few months. I'm baking the cake for her," Sage, according to her nametag, added.

"I bet it'll be the best cake ever," I told Avery.

"It will. I know it." She turned to her mom. "Mom, can I have a donut?"

Sage frowned down at her. "You've already had one and a half."

"But I'm hungry," she complained, holding her stomach for emphasis.

Sage tapped a pen to her chin in thought, then said, "Half of one. But only if you promise to go back to your drawing table."

"Okay!" Avery agreed.

Sage slid open the glass door and grabbed the donut with pink icing, ripping it in half and handing one side to Avery. She grabbed it from her and ran back through the doors, crumbs falling to the ground in her wake.

"Want a free half of a donut?" Sage asked, sliding the bakery cabinet doors closed.

I laughed. "Sure. And one black coffee to go, please." Lennon liked it black, I knew that much. The distinct smell of black coffee lingered in his office every time I walked by. I'd know if he was a creamer kind of guy.

She placed the donut in a brown paper bag and folded the top, then turned to grab an empty cup and filled it with rich coffee. The scent invaded my nose, making me wish I'd give in and use some of the cash Lennon gave me for a coffee of my own.

"You don't peg me for a black coffee kind of gal," Sage observed as she set the cup on the counter in front of me.

"Oh, it's not for me. I'm a latte girl through and through."

She smiled, her dark lashes casting a shadow over her cheeks as she typed the total into the register. "Two dollars."

I pulled the wad of cash from my pocket, taking four dollar bills out. I handed her two, then placed the other two in the tip jar. Lennon seemed like a tipper. He'd appreciate it.

"I'm Sage, by the way. That tornado of a child is my daughter, Avery," she said after closing the register drawer.

"Oakley," I offered, grabbing the coffee and bag.

"Are you new to town? I haven't seen you around."

"I am. I'm working at Tumbleweed Feed down the block."

"Lennon's a great guy, but I'm sure he's an even better boss," she said, really putting the emphasis on how small of a town this was.

I gave a closed-lip smile, remembering how he'd stood up for me in front of that customer the other day who tried to tip me a quarter.

"Thanks for the coffee and half donut," I said.

She grinned. "Of course. Come on in anytime."

Once I had money, I'd definitely be doing that. Nothing cheered me up like a vanilla latte on ice.

Making my way out of the store, I hurried down the main street to Tumbleweed Feed. It felt weird going in there on my day off, but I had no choice. I didn't want to keep his money longer than I had to.

I passed closed shop doors with bright lights glowing inside, lighting up the sidewalk on this overcast day. I could practically feel the heat coming from the inside of the stores as I walked, but it did little to ease my nerves at seeing Lennon after last night.

I couldn't believe I'd asked if he was going to try to sleep with me. I was his employee, for crying out loud. He probably thought I was just some typical girl trying to get into any guy's pants that paid me the slightest bit of attention. Plus, he probably only helped me get home safe because he didn't want to lose another employee.

That was definitely it.

Swinging open the door, I stepped in, the heat immediately licking at my frozen fingers. My hand around his hot coffee had stayed relatively warm, but my other hand was practically an ice cube.

"Oakley? What are you doing here?" Leo asked from the shelf where he was stocking dog food cans.

"Is Lennon here?" I didn't want to stay long. I had a busy day ahead of me that included curling under the covers, throwing on a movie, and napping.

"Right here," Lennon's deep voice announced, coming out of one of the aisles.

I closed the distance, shoving the coffee and bag at his chest. "Here."

He didn't move to grab them. Instead, he just stared down at me with a blank face.

"Can you take these so I can get your cash out?"

He crossed his arms, still not taking the damn coffee. He'd be lucky if this didn't end up all over his work shirt. Then he'd be forced to take it off, and I'd have no choice but to drool over what I had the biggest feeling laid beneath the fabric.

Maybe I should dump the coffee.

"That's yours. I left it for you," he said grumpily.

Thinking it best to get this damn cup out of my hand, I set it on the end cap next to me, then shoved my hand into my pocket, fishing out the money. "I don't want your charity."

"It's not charity. I'm doing you a favor."

My jaw dropped before I could stop it. A favor? Is that what he thought he was doing, just giving me money out of the kindness of his heart? My dad did that, and he controlled me with it. I wouldn't take any handouts anymore. I'd work in a goddamn coal mine and never see the light of day if I had to.

I set the cash next to his coffee on the metal shelf, but kept my fingers gripped on the bag. "I'm keeping the half of this donut."

"Half? You get hungry on the way over?" The corners of his lips inched up the slightest bit as he fought a smile, while the corners of my mouth turned down.

"No. Sage gave it to me because Avery wanted half and-" I shut my mouth, closing my eyes and inhaling a deep breath. "You know what?" My eyes opened, landing on his chest. "It doesn't matter. Have a good rest of your day. I'll be here tomorrow."

I turned on my heel and headed for the door, not slowing my pace or bothering to look back.

I was ready for my day of relaxation, and being in Lennon's presence made me feel anything but tranquil.

12

OAKLEY

My fingers fumbled with the hem of my burgundy Tumbleweed Feed long sleeve, adjusting it back over my stomach after pulling my sweatshirt off in the break room. My day off consisted of napping, overthinking, and shivering. I'd been able to sleep when I got home after my coffee and cash drop off, but once the outside air seeped into the old house I was renting, the temperatures were too cold to sleep through.

Forced to lay there in my own thoughts while curling up in a ball under the blankets on the couch, I'd debated driving back to Denver. It was the last thing I wanted to do, but if I didn't go before the first snow, I'd have no choice but to stay here at least until spring.

It was too dangerous to drive those icy roads all the way from Idaho to Colorado with bald tires. Plus, with my terrible driving record, there was no way I'd make it there in one piece. After much thought, I came to the conclusion that staying was my best bet. I was all too quick to remind myself that I'd left home for a reason, and being miserable in my tiny, cold bungalow made me somewhat forget about those reasons.

There was no way I'd go back to my father acting the way he was just for a heated house. I'd take negative temperatures over hearing him complain for hours on end about my mom.

It wasn't that I didn't want to be there for him and hear his side of things, but I was at the point that, with him trying to get me to cut my mom off completely, I couldn't handle it anymore. They loved each other, had a family together, and while cheating was extremely unacceptable, I wouldn't put my family through the ringer for someone else's mistakes.

What happened between my dad and mom should be between them. They shouldn't be involving me in the crossfire because they thought I'd be the end all to their argument with which parents' side I would take. I loved them both equally.

Pinning my name tag above my right breast, I headed out to the floor.

"Oakley." Lennon's voice filled the hallway as I was almost past his office.

Stopping in my tracks, I poked my head in his office, not passing the door jam. "Yes?"

"I have something for you," he said, not looking up from his computer.

Oh, God, please don't be more of his money.

Taking that as he wanted me to come in, I hesitantly walked to the chair across from him and sat. "Listen, about yesterday-"

He tossed an envelope on the desk in front of me, cutting me off and finally meeting my gaze. My eyes flicked to the white envelope, then back to him. "What's that?"

"Advance on your paycheck," he said with no emotion whatsoever.

I didn't reach for it. "You didn't need to do that."

"Seemed like you needed it." *Needed* it. Like I was some poor girl desperate for cash.

"I don't need extra handouts." I tried to keep the annoyance out of my tone, but it was proving difficult.

"It's not necessarily a handout. It would've been your money anyway."

"How do you know I'm not going to quit?"

He raised an eyebrow. "Are you?"

"Well, no."

He leaned back in his chair, his posture the perfect picture of relaxed.

"The cash, now this. I don't need your pity, Lennon."

He crossed his arms. "Is me caring about you having food to eat really pity, though?"

"It's a form of it."

And it showed he cared, which is what I didn't want. I knew I was trying to keep him away because of my current situation, but what good would that do me?

"If me giving you your paycheck early so that you can eat real food is what makes you hate me, then loathe me all you want. But it's not going to deter me." His gaze hardened a moment before he unfolded his arms and went back to looking at his computer.

Instead of fighting him more, I said, "Thank you for driving me home from the bar the other night."

"It was a lot more than a drive, Oak." My cheeks flushed, heat creeping up my neck, arms, and every other limb. The effect Lennon had on me was criminal.

"Right. You walked me inside." I leaned forward and grabbed the envelope, then stood. "Need anything else before I go out there?"

His gaze raked over my body before landing back on my face. "No." But his eyes said otherwise.

***

Today was my first day alone on the floor. Jacey and Leo both had the day off, so it was just me and Lennon here. I did my best to balance the customers while stocking shelves, facing products, and refilling treat containers at the front. Any time a small problem arose, I'd try to figure it out on my own before jumping to ask Lennon for help. He'd been in his office all morning, but I had seen him come out to the floor a few times and get stopped by a local.

An hour before closing, I had my back to the front door as I poured the treats into the glass jar, and I must've not heard the bell on the door ding, because the voice behind me startled me. "Getting ready for lunch?"

I jumped, spinning around to come face to face with a middle-aged man. Beneath his jacket, I could tell he was a little pudgy around the middle. His five o'clock shadow had some gray mixed in with the brunette hairs, matching the messed up strands on his head.

"What?" I asked, confused by what he meant.

"Those treats. They smell good."

I awkwardly smiled, taking a step back to give myself some space from him. "They're pumpkin cinnamon flavored. Dogs love them."

"Ah, so they're for the dogs. Not scooby snacks."

Scooby snacks?

"Uh, yeah," I said quietly, not sure what else to say to that.

"I'm referring to the scooby snacks for people, not the dog in the show," he said, itching his forearm. "Anyway, I was wondering if you could recommend a good brand of dog food for my puppy?"

Putting his comment to the side, I smiled. "Of course. Come with me."

I led him over to the dog food aisle, his feet just a step behind me. Bringing him over to one of our more popular brands, I pulled a small bag down from the top shelf and turned to show him the list of ingredients. "Alana Farms' first ingredient on their list is always a protein, which is what you want to aim for when trying to find a good dog food brand. You don't want some filler like a legume or grain as the first few ingredients."

He grabbed the bag from me, reading the list. "Why's that?"

"Well, the first few ingredients are what the kibble is primarily made of, and a dog, especially a high energy puppy, should have an abundance of protein in their diet."

He tossed the bag from one hand to the other, examining the front. "You sound like a spokesperson."

I shrugged. "Salesperson, spokesperson."

"That's cool that you know your stuff," he said with a grin.

"I like to study up on it so that when people like you ask, I know what I'm talking about."

"Smart girl. I like it."

I cleared my throat, looking at the other bags on the shelf around me. "Was there anything else you needed for your puppy?"

"What else do you need for a puppy besides food?" he joked.

I let out an awkward laugh that was too breathy and picked at a piece of lint on the sleeve of my shirt. "Toys, treats-"

"I've got a lot of toys at home."

Pursing my lips together, I hesitated a moment. I was sure he meant dog toys, but there was something else in his tone that indicated he wasn't just talking about the canine variety.

"I can ring you up if you're ready," I said, looking for an out.

He stepped one foot to the side and waved his hand out, gesturing me to go first. I stepped around him, making my way up to the register and coming around the back of it. As I reached for the small bag of kibble he set on the counter, my eyes caught on Lennon facing a shelf with a clipboard and pen in his hand.

Scanning the bag, I checked the total for the man's transaction, then read it off to him.

He pulled out his wallet and took out a card, inserting it into the payment terminal.

"So you said you study at home," he said as he waited for the payment to go through.

Technically, I'd just said I study. He was the one to mention the home part.

"Yep."

"What side of town do you live on?" he asked, like it was casual conversation to ask retail workers where they lived.

The receipt printed out as the POS dinged for him to remove his card. "Uh..."

"Oakley, I need your help with price checks." Lennon's voice interrupted the sound of the printer and the abundance of thoughts racing through my head on how to answer the guy. I didn't want to be rude and say *none of your business,* but why the hell would I tell him where I live?

My gaze shot up to Lennon, who still had his clipboard and pen in hand, but instead of studying numbers on labels stuck to shelves, he was studying me like he could see my discomfort written on my face.

"Got it," I said to him, then brought my attention back to the customer. "Sorry, duty calls." I offered a half-smile, hoping it would ease over how I hadn't answered his question. I had no interest in getting to know the guy, so I wasn't eager to answer personal questions like that.

"Retail, am I right?" he joked.

My lips thinned as I gave him a nod. "Yep. Hope your puppy likes the food."

"I'll keep you updated." He grabbed the bag and exited the store, but instead of joining Lennon, I stayed put, inhaling a deep breath. I hadn't realized I'd been taking such short breaths during the interaction with the guy, and my lungs ached with the need for more oxygen.

"You okay?" Lennon asked from where he stood, a deep line in between his brows.

"Yep," I replied, pulling myself out of my thoughts and making my way over to him.

Lennon kept his eyes on me the entire short walk over to him. "That man say something to you?"

"Nope," I squeaked. "You needed my help with price checks?"

He clipped his pen on the paper attached to his clipboard and dropped it to his side. "No."

Confusion rolled through me as he turned and walked back to his office, where he disappeared to until the end of the day. Lennon baffled me with his back and forth, and it pissed me off that I wanted to be the one to crack his hard exterior.

13

LENNON

The desire to close my office door was overpowered by the need to listen for Oakley out on the sales floor. I'd heard the man say something about toys to her from my office and immediately stormed out to the floor with my price sheet in hand to make it look like I had a reason to be out there.

The moment Oakley came around the end of the aisle, I knew something was off. Her movements were stiff, her shoulders slightly slumped. Gone was the sunshine that radiated off her like the sunrise after a long winter's night. I didn't know exactly what the guy said, but it took all I had in me not to kick him out of my store. I hadn't gotten a good look at his face to know him the next time he came in, which pissed me off even more.

She hadn't wanted to open up to me about what he said, which I didn't expect her to, but it still made my blood boil. Not wanting to show how aggravated I was, I returned to my office, where I planned to get lost in payroll and schedules for my three employees.

Now that Oakley was here, I could give Jacey and Leo more days off, but that meant she'd be alone most of the day on the floor if she was scheduled with me. Though I didn't want her being alone all day out there, I didn't want to schedule her with the others. As much work as I had to get done, I savored the small glimpses of her.

I could look, but not touch, right?

To not raise any suspicion, I scheduled her a couple days with Jacey and Leo, and the rest with me. That was fair enough. The manager should be in the building with his new employee to make sure she didn't screw anything up.

Yeah. That was it.

My computer pinged with an email and I moved the cursor on the screen to open it, seeing that it was from the rental company that owned this building.

> Good morning,
> I understand you'd like to close out the lease on the building you rent from us and purchase the property. As you still have two years left of the contract, it is in our best interest to see through the duration of the terms initially discussed. At

this time, we are not looking to sell the building, but our prior discussion of the increased rate applies.
Best,
Alfred

"*Best,* my ass," I muttered. There had to be a way to fight this with his company. I wasn't going to pay increased rent on a building I could own and pay less on each month. If he wanted to stick to the initial duration in our original contract, then he'd have to stick with the agreed payments, not a penny more.

I shot back an email and almost broke my mouse clicking the send button. After I sent the email, I worked on finalizing next week's schedule, then printed it out on a piece of paper to post in the break room.

Grabbing the paper from the printer, I stood and headed for the break room, but before I could even take a step outside my office, my chest collided with a small, soft form.

The paper floated to the ground after I dropped it to steady the redhead in front of me.

"Shit, sorry," Oakley mumbled, bending to pick up the paper.

With us just having collided, she was too close to me as she bent down. Her ponytail fell over her shoulder, the ends brushing my jeans as she stood with the schedule in her hand. I bit the inside of my cheek to keep any thoughts from rushing from one head to the other.

It should be illegal for a woman like Oakley to wear a ponytail like that, all high and perky, all of her hair swishing with every movement she made. A few of the strands had made their way loose throughout the day, framing her cheekbones and rosy cheeks.

I grabbed the paper from her and made no move to step back. I was the one leaving my office after all. If she wanted space between us, she could be the one to move.

Those green eyes darted past me to my office before settling back on my face. "I'm ready to go if you are," she said.

Glancing at the watch on my wrist, I noticed it was fifteen minutes past closing. Did I really lose track of time?

"Let me close up and then we can go. Did you lock the front?" The last thing I needed right now was some straggler customer coming in for a last minute purchase and making me have to stay later than necessary.

"Yeah."

I waited for her to move, but she just kept standing there like she lost the ability to control her limbs.

"Are you going to let me by?" I grumbled. If I had to, I'd move her myself.

Thinking of my hands on her did things to my body that I did not want to feel. Not when it came to Oakley. I was eight years older than her, for crying out loud.

Her eyes stayed trained on the band of my hat across my forehead. "I thought we talked about that," she whispered.

Again with the whispering.

My brows drew together. I thought the thing about the hat at the bar was a joke. I honestly hadn't even realized it was backwards. I must've turned it around when I was frustrated as all get out at the rental guy.

"If you want it back, just say the words." I'd gladly give it to her if that's what she wanted. Any excuse to see her wearing it again was a good one.

"I'd much rather you keep it."

I invaded her space just a *little* more, and to my surprise, she didn't move away. "Keep it like this?" I asked, my voice low.

Her eyes met mine as she swallowed, our chests barely touching as we both breathed each other in.

In a flash, she jumped out of whatever stupor she was lost in and took one massive step backwards. Finally able to move, I disappeared into the break room, slid the schedule into the clear sleeve taped to the wall, and passed back by Oakley in the hall to get the till from the register.

When I came back, she was still standing there, but now she was leaning against the wall, her hands behind her back. I brought the drawer full of cash to my desk, counted it twice, and zipped away the extra in a bag for the bank drop. Leaving two hundred dollars in the drawer, I locked it away in the safe, then powered down my computer and stood.

Oakley was still stuck to the wall, staring at something on the floor. I checked around my feet to be sure she wasn't struck speechless by a rat running around or something, and found nothing. Grabbing the keys off my desk, I closed my office door behind me, the only light in the building coming from the front of the store.

"You got your things?" I asked her.

She nodded and I narrowed my eyes at her. Against my better judgment, I approached her, setting one hand on the wall above her head. "Cat got your tongue, Oak?"

I knew what I was doing to her. Whatever was up with her wasn't just about my damn hat, but I didn't care. Oakley was awestruck right now, and the look on her face only made me want to keep it going.

She tilted her chin up to look at me, her eyes darting to the band of my hat resting on my forehead, then back to me.

"I could give you something to talk about, but I think that mouth has better things to do than talk." I was playing a dangerous game, but with Oakley, danger seemed a little fun. I should *not* be crossing this line right now, but seeing her frazzled just did something to me.

Her lips parted and her cheeks instantly flushed. My eyes flicked to the deep shade of crimson, noting the freckles that dotted her nose, then I pushed away from her and the wall like nothing happened.

"Time to go, Oak," I said.

She snapped her jaw shut and turned, heading for the front of the store.

Oakley was a blazing distraction to have around here, but fuck if I didn't want to poke the fire.

14

OAKLEY

Snowflakes fell from the sky outside the windows of the feed store, coating the sidewalk in a fluffy layer of white snow. My denim jacket was layered over my long sleeve despite the heat inside the building. Just looking at the snow made me cold.

If I'd just wear Lennon's coat, this wouldn't be a problem.

No, Oakley. Don't be stupid. You're giving that back to him...eventually.

I'd seen it hanging on my coat rack every day since, but couldn't get the nerve to wear it or give it back. I was conflicted over a damn *jacket*.

It'd been four days since Lennon stood above me in the hall looking every bit mouthwatering. Since then, I'd avoided him at all costs. I didn't know what got into him that night, but whatever it was, it was contagious, because I'd wanted nothing more than for him to kiss me against that wall.

There was no more trying to deny the fact that I was attracted to Lennon. Seeing that primal look come over his face as he stared down at me did something to my core, and I wanted to feel it again.

But for the sake of our work environment, it shouldn't happen again.

The bell on the door dinged, and I swiveled to see Margaret, an elderly woman who had lived in town for eighty-two years and ran the knitting club, walking through the door. She'd been in here once this week already to pick up bird seed and talked my ear off, but she was sweet and reminded me of my grandma, so I welcomed the conversation.

"Good morning, Margaret," I greeted.

"Well, hello, sweetie. Good day so far?" she croaked.

"As good as it can get. Bit slow because of the snow, but I'm not mad about it."

Her thin lips painted pink widened into a smile. "Can't complain about a little quiet."

Coming around the register, I asked, "Is there anything I can grab for you?"

She waved me off, continuing her slow gait toward the small animal aisle. "Just need some nuts for the squirrels."

I smiled, a warmth spreading through my chest. What was it with elderly people wanting to feed the entire forest?

"Well, I'll be up here if you need me."

Margaret liked to do things herself. Her words the other day were, "I may be old, but I ain't dead yet."

As she disappeared down the aisle, the bell dinged again. I turned to greet the customer, but stopped when I saw who it was.

Scooby Snack Guy.

"Good morning," he greeted.

"Morning. Did your puppy like the food?"

He shook the snow off his beanie before placing it back on his head. "Loved it. I'm actually here to get more if you have some."

I nodded. "Lennon always keeps it in stock. It's a favorite around here. I can grab it for you."

He waved me off, just like Margaret. "I've got it."

He disappeared down the dog food aisle just as Margaret reappeared, bag of nuts in hand. "I'm ready to pay, dear."

Going back around the register, I scanned the bag after she set it down on the counter. "Are you out driving in that snow?"

She set her purse on the counter and slowly unzipped it to pull out her wallet. "A little snow never hurt anyone. Don't worry about me. I've been living here for eighty-two years and never had a problem with the snow."

She handed me cash and I counted it out, entering the amount into the register. The drawer popped open on a ding and I grabbed her change. "Do you have someone at home waiting for you?" I couldn't help but worry about an old woman driving in the snow.

"Yes, dear. My sweet husband, Carl. He's always waiting for me," she replied as she slipped the coins into her little coin purse.

I closed the drawer and handed her the receipt. "Alright. You drive safe, okay? It's slippery out there."

She slung her purse back over her shoulder and picked up her bag of nuts. "I'm always safe. How do you think I made it to be this old?"

I smiled as she turned to head out the door, pulling her hood up with one hand.

"Carl passed away five years ago," a male voice said.

Taking my eyes off Margaret walking to her car out the window, I found Scooby Snack Guy standing across from me. "He did?"

He nodded, setting the small bag of kibble on the counter. "I'm not sure if she forgets sometimes, but I know she misses him. Everyone does. My mom goes to her knitting group and she talks about him all the time."

Thinking about losing a loved one so close to you and being alone hit me like a punch to the chest. I cleared the emotion from my throat and grabbed the bag to scan it.

"You know we have bigger bags of this, right?" I asked.

"I saw them," he replied.

"If you buy a bigger bag, you won't have to come in as often," I pointed out.

He shrugged. "I don't mind the drive. Gets me out of the house."

The total came up on the payment terminal and he inserted his card.

The silence as it processed the payment was awkward, so I asked the first question that came to mind. "How long have you had your puppy?"

"About two weeks now. I got her when she was eight weeks."

"That's the best stage. What breed is she?"

"Chihuahua. I rescued her from the pound," he said as the terminal beeped for him to remove his card.

"She must be so tiny."

He nodded. "She is." He slipped the card back into his wallet and pocketed it. "Do you have any pets?"

I shook my head, handing him the receipt. "No. I just moved here and don't really have time for a dog right now."

He grabbed the bag and held it by his side. "You should get one. You know a lot about this stuff."

"Maybe," I said, thinking about a dog to come home to. Maybe I wouldn't feel as lonely then.

"Get home safe later, Oakley. Roads are getting bad out there."

I internally frowned at the use of my name, silently cursing the name tag pinned to my shirt. On the outside, I smiled. "Thanks, I will."

He headed out of the store as I stood there, dreading having to stay through the rest of my shift. The weather forecasted it would be snowing into the night, which meant the roads would only get worse, and my tires were not ready for ice or snow.

I hadn't had the chance to buy chains yet, and I was cursing myself for not forking up the money and buying them sooner.

Lennon wasn't here today either, which was somehow making the day go by even slower. I was scheduled with Jacey who'd been unloading freight from our recent shipment all morning. Leaning an elbow on the counter, I blew a stray hair from my face. If I just didn't look at the clock, it'd go by quickly.

If only it worked that way.

***

Six o'clock did not come quickly, despite my efforts to not watch the time. Business had been slow all day, so I'd been helping Jacey put out products near the front so I could simultaneously keep an eye on the register.

I found Jacey in the office counting out the money for the safe and leaned against the door jam with my hands in my coat pockets.

"The first snow always keeps people inside, but it'll pick up. They'll all get in the groove of driving on the roads again," she said.

"Thank God. I thought being busy was hard, but having no customers just made the day lag."

"Like keeping busy?" she asked, bending to shove the bag in the safe with the till.

"Busy means I have no time to think about the other stuff going on in my life," I replied. It was true. When there were customers needing my help left and right, I had no time to think about my parents, but today, I had thought of them constantly.

"I totally get that," she said, standing to pull on her coat and grab her purse. "I know you're from Denver and all, but are you going to be okay driving in the snow?"

"Yeah, I'll be okay. Are you?"

She nodded as we headed to the front of the store side by side. "Yeah. Lived here my whole life. I'm used to it."

Jacey punched a code into the alarm and we stepped out the door. She turned to lock up the store behind us before we crossed the parking lot to our cars. The snow was up over the toe of my sneaker, the cold licking at my ankles. It had to be a good three to four inches already.

"Lennon's not always like that," she said.

I stopped by the rear of my car as she unlocked her own, tossing her purse on the seat.

"Like what?" I asked.

"Grumpy, closed off, irritable. Deep down, he's like.." She searched for the word. "A teddy bear."

A laugh escaped my lips. "A teddy bear, huh?"

She smiled. "Yeah. He's sweet on the inside. Just give him some time and he'll warm up."

I tipped my chin, toeing at the snow. "I'll take your word for it."

"Now get home, it's freezing out here. I'll see you on our next shift."

"See ya." I came around my car to the driver's side and slid in. I locked my doors and started the car, cranking the heater as high as it would go. Jacey pulled out of the parking lot as I waited for my car to heat up enough to be able to move my limbs to drive.

Checking the dash, the temperature read seventeen degrees out. How in the fuck was it that cold already? Wasn't it just fall? Then again, summer quickly turned to winter in the west, leaving maybe a day or two to feel like fall in between.

Finally warm enough that I could feel my fingers, I shifted into reverse and slowly eased the car back. I tapped the brakes and it stopped, giving me hope that I could make it home in one piece.

Shifting into drive, I pulled out of the parking lot and onto the main road. There was no one out on the roads or sidewalks, the low temperatures and almost blizzard-like conditions keeping them home.

I'd have no choice but to run my heater tonight. I'd freeze to death in my sleep if I didn't, and the last thing I wanted was for my parents to get a call that I'd died of frostbite in my bed because I didn't have enough money to run the heater.

Turning onto the next road, my back end slid a little and I felt my heart flutter in my chest. As soon as it felt like it was going to keep sliding, the car straightened itself out and picked up traction again.

I let out a sigh of relief, but it was all too soon, because the moment I thought I was fine, I wasn't. My car's rear end slid again and on instinct, I slammed the brakes, which made it worse.

Never slam the brakes in the snow, Oakley.

My rear end fish-tailed and the front of my car dove head first into a ditch, my body slamming against my seat belt as gravity shoved me forward. My engine sputtered, and then silence filled my ears as the lights on my dash disappeared.

15

LENNON

"You could always sue the guy," Reed pointed out.

"For what?" Callan spewed after swallowing his sip of beer.

Reed crossed a boot over the other, leaning back in his chair at the table that sat on his covered porch. It was snowing, but the space heater kept us warm enough. "For breaking the contract. He wants to break the contract by raising the rent, but then says you need to stick by the original contract and continue leasing for another couple years? Bullshit."

"I'm not going to sue him, guys," I said.

"Why not?" they asked in unison.

"That's a whole lot of paperwork, and money, and time. All of which I either don't have or don't want to do." Once you got lawyers involved, things got ugly. Worst case scenario, I'd just ride the length of the lease and purchase the building at the end. I didn't want to do that, but if he wasn't going to budge, I didn't really have a choice.

The last thing I wanted to do was piss him off and have him kick my business out.

"Don't we know any lawyers?" Callan asked.

Reed scoffed. "No, idiot, because we aren't smart enough to know any lawyers."

"Not the fact that we live in a town with barely five hundred people?" I asked.

Reed took a swig of his beer as Rouge, Lettie and Bailey's Australian Shepherd, came running around the side of the house. "What the hell are you doing over here, Rouge?"

The dog came up to me, setting his front two paws on my thigh as he begged for chest rubs. "If he's over here, that means Bailey and Lettie are distracted," I pointed out.

"Gross," Callan muttered.

Reed finished off his beer, then tossed it in the trash can he kept by his back porch. "That dog know how to fetch a beer?"

I chuckled. "Rouge thinks he has a tail, Reed. You really think he's smart enough to go get you a beer from the fridge?"

"He must've got his brain from us," Callan said.

Reed stood from his chair. "I'm getting another. You guys want one?"

I shook my head. "I'm good. I have to drive home, and it's snowing."

"This heater must be industrial strength or something, Reed. Where'd you get it?" Callan asked.

"Mom bought it," he grumbled as he headed inside.

Rouge curled up next to the heater, relishing in the heat as it melted the snow off his fur. At this point, Rouge was everyone's dog. His love for people was too much for his own good.

My phone buzzed in my back pocket, vibrating against the chair. I twisted, pulling it out. My brows furrowed as I saw Oakley's name lit up on my screen. Why would she be calling me at six-thirty at night?

I tapped the button to answer and held the phone to my ear. "Oak?"

"Hey, Lennon. Uh, sorry to call you, but I don't really have anyone else's number around here besides Lettie and you were the first person I thought of that might know what to do. I don't want to inconvenience you though, so if you're busy, I get it-"

"Oak, what's wrong?" I interrupted her. She was babbling, but I could hear the slight shake to her voice.

Callan straightened beside me, watching me on the phone.

"My car slid off the road."

I shot to my feet, abandoning my beer on the table. "Are you okay?"

"Depends what you mean by 'okay.'"

"Where are you?"

"Uh." Her teeth chattered through the phone with her pause. She must've been looking at her surroundings, trying to figure out where she was. That didn't comfort me one fucking bit. "I don't really know. Can I send you my location?"

"Send it now," I instructed.

"On the phone with you?"

"Yes, Oakley. So I can make sure I get it."

"Okay, uh, hold on." She pulled the phone away from her ear, and the call was silent. There wasn't a single sound coming through until my phone dinged with her text. I glanced at the screen to be safe that I got her exact location, and then held it back to my ear.

"I'll be there soon. Stay in the car."

"Okay," she said, her voice quivering with the cold.

I hung up and shoved my phone back in my jeans as Reed came through the porch door. "What's got your face all contorted?"

"Oakley drove off the road," I explained briefly before taking the porch steps three at a time to go around his house for my truck in the driveway.

I started it up, wasting no time letting it warm up, but I did crank the heater to fight off the chill. It was too damn cold out there for her to be on the side of the road, and the snow was coming down relentlessly.

I sped down the driveway, my snow tires gripping the road like it was a warm summer day instead of almost-blizzard like conditions, and headed toward the location Oakley had sent me.

She better be okay. She had to be.

16

OAKLEY

With the heater, and the rest of my car, currently not running, the cold quickly seeped into the vehicle. It penetrated my skin through my jacket, wracking a shiver out of me. I cursed myself for not keeping Lennon's jacket in my car as a backup layer in case something like this did happen. You could never be too prepared in the winter.

I was definitely not prepared to slide off the road. But then again, who was?

My fingers hid in my sleeves, trying to find warmth in the fabric, but I snuck one hand out to grab my phone and check the time. Twelve minutes. That was how long it'd been since I got off the phone with Lennon. I wasn't sure where he was when he answered, but I hoped he'd be here soon.

I felt pathetic calling him to come to my rescue, but his number was the only one in my phone that didn't belong to someone in Denver aside from Lettie, and I didn't want to drag her into this mess. I could have walked home from here and called a tow truck, but I didn't exactly know my way around Bell Buckle yet, and my sneakers weren't meant to trudge through the snow.

Dropping my phone back in the cup holder, I tried to crank the key again, but nothing happened. The car acted like it wanted to start but just couldn't get there. On the third try, I dropped my hand, retreating my fingers back into my sleeve.

Headlights lit up my car, causing me to look up. I shielded my eyes as I saw the vehicle slow to a stop on the side of the road near my car. Hoping it was Lennon, I grabbed the handle on my driver door and shoved it open. Snow fell on my legs from where it had piled on top of my car, but I didn't care. All I could think about was getting out of here and getting warm.

My feet didn't touch the ground like they typically did when I swung them out, which caused me to look down. In the dim light of the other vehicle, I could see that my car was at such an angle that the ground was about a foot beneath me.

Figuring there was no other way to get out, I made the small jump, my feet burying in the snow. Icicles shot up my legs, causing me to set a hand on the door to steady myself. The icy substance instantly froze my feet more than they already were, seeping in the holes where the laces were.

Making space, I swung my door shut and eyed the embankment. I didn't have a choice but to use my hands to climb up the slippery slope. Otherwise I'd just slide down on my feet.

I started to clamber up, trying to find leverage in the snow, but finding it difficult with frozen fingers.

I needed to buy some fucking gloves. And chains. And snow boots. And a warmer jacket. Just all of it. I needed all of it.

"You okay over there?" a male voice called from the rear end of my vehicle. Unfortunately, it wasn't Lennon, but he had to be here soon, right?

"Down here!" I shouted through my struggle up the snow.

The man's silhouette appeared as my hand gripped the top of the slope. "Shit, let me help you."

A gloved hand gripped my bare one and pulled me up the rest of the way. I scrambled to my feet, having a hard time getting my balance with my frozen toes.

"T-thank you," I said through a shiver.

"You drive off the road?" he asked. His voice sounded familiar, but with everything that just happened, I couldn't figure out where I'd heard it before.

"S-slid on i-ice." My arms wrapped around my torso in a poor attempt to warm myself up more.

"Gotta be careful on these icy roads. They sneak up on ya," he said.

Another set of headlights came into view, lighting up the man's face. He was wearing a beanie, but I recognized his face.

Scooby Snack Guy.

BEAT AROUND THE BUSH

The now-familiar rumble of Lennon's engine filled my ears as he pulled over. He'd barely put the truck in park before he was jumping out and storming towards me. If I didn't know him, I'd be scared. Hell, Scooby Snack Guy should be.

About five feet from me, keeping his stride, he pulled off his jacket. Once he was close enough that I had to look up at him, he wrapped the jacket around my shoulders, pulling it tight in the front.

"Get in the truck," Lennon demanded.

"My phone-" I'd left it in my car.

"I'll get it. Get in the truck," he repeated. Even in the dim light, I could tell he wouldn't take no for an answer, and thankfully for him, I didn't have the energy to fight. Plus, he'd kept his truck running, which meant the heater was on, and all I wanted right now was a little bit of warmth.

"O-okay," I managed to get out before I made the slow trek to the passenger side of his truck.

"Do you know her?" Scooby Snack Guy asked from somewhere behind me.

I couldn't hear Lennon's response as my feet shuffled through the snow.

"How do I know you're not going to hurt her?" the guy asked.

I paused, twisting slightly so I could see them.

This time, I heard Lennon loud and clear.

"I didn't see you trying to help her, so if anyone's intentions here should be questioned, it's yours. Now get the fuck out of my way so I can take care of my girl."

My girl?

I turned back around as Lennon disappeared down the embankment. If I wasn't so damn cold, every nerve in my body would be on fire right now. *He'd called me his girl.* Maybe it was because he was worried and it slipped out, but he'd said it with no hesitation. There was no way he really thought that about me.

I wasn't sure how long it took, but he was back right as I reached the door with my phone in his hand.

He reached around me, pulling the handle. My movements were slow with the cold as I reached for the door to pull myself in. He rested a hand on my back, giving me the extra gentle push I needed to plop down in the seat.

"It's s-so w-warm," I mumbled as the uncontrollable shivers wracked through me.

"I know, Oak. Let me get in." He closed the passenger door and a second later, he was sliding into the driver's side, slamming his door shut.

"Scoot closer," he instructed.

I tried to get my footing on the floor to scoot into the middle seat, but my feet were so numb, I could barely put any pressure on them. "My f-feet."

His gaze moved to my shoes and he cursed, reaching over to pull me closer. He was so warm. His hands, his body, everything about Lennon right now was fire, and I was stuck in an iceberg.

He reached around my waist, buckling me in, and then wrapped an arm around my shoulders, pulling me into him. My head fell to his shoulder as my conscience screamed at me to lift it. I breathed him in and nuzzled further into his neck.

"Fuck, Oak. You're frozen," he said as my nose touched the skin on his neck.

"I'm s-sorry," I whispered, unable to speak any louder as I continued to shake. Somewhere in front of us, headlights moved, but I was too cold to care about the guy.

He shifted into drive, not bothering with his own seat belt. I was blocking the buckle anyway, and while I was all about safety first, I didn't want to move even an inch away from him right now.

My eyes drifted shut with the lull of the engine, but his hand started rubbing my shoulder, keeping me from drifting off completely. "Stay awake for me, Oak. We're almost there."

"W-where?"

"My house."

His house?

If I wasn't so damned cold right now, I'd demand he take me to mine, but seeing as though the heater in my house hadn't been running all day, it'd take hours for it to warm up if I turned it on now. I didn't know how quick frostbite set in, but I got the feeling his house was already warm, so I'd accept my fate until I was warm enough to go home.

A few turns later, he shut off the engine. "You want to slide out on my side?" he asked.

I nodded, my cheek rubbing against his shoulder with the motion.

God, he smelled good.

He reached around to unbuckle my seat belt, and then the door opened, his warmth abandoning me. I almost whimpered at the loss of his body next to mine, but before I had the chance to, large hands gripped my hands and helped scoot me to the edge of the bench seat.

"I'm going to carry you, okay?"

"Okay."

One arm wrapped around my back, the other right behind my knees, and then I was floating. My cheek rested against his hard chest, his jacket swallowing me up in his arms.

I heard a jingle of keys, a lock click, and a door swing open. As we crossed the threshold, blissful warmth surrounded my body. He closed the door with his boot and flicked a light on, then brought me down the hall.

"Your house is nice," I mumbled, even though I'd barely gotten a look.

A second later, I was laid down on a soft, plush surface, and his fingers were gently grabbing my ankle as his other hand unlaced my sneaker. Once the first one was off, he started on the other.

"Your socks are soaked," he said, more to himself than to me. I was well aware of the state my feet were in, given I could barely feel them at the moment.

He got the second shoe off, tossing it to the floor. "I need to take your pants off, Oak. They're wet."

"I don't have any other pants," I said as another shiver wracked my body, even though the house was warm.

"I have some sweats you can borrow. Lift your hips." His fingers worked at the button on my jeans, then I heard the zipper, and his skin brushed mine as he hooked his fingers in the waistband. I did my best to lift, giving him an inch of space. But with muscles like that, that was all he needed to pull my pants off completely.

God, how I wished this was happening under different circumstances.

Instead of clothing me with those sweats he mentioned, he pulled the covers over me, and then came around to the other side of the bed and crawled in beside me. As his legs touched mine, I realized he'd taken his pants off as well, and by the bareness of his arms, he'd lost his shirt, too.

"While I'd l-love to s-sleep with you right now, I'm too t-tired," I mumbled into the soft pillow.

His arm snaked around my waist, his head just above mine on the pillow. "I'm not trying to sleep with you, Oak. I'm trying to get you warm."

My frozen feet found his warm skin, but he didn't pull away. He let me use his heat to warm me up. His entire body against mine made every nerve ending in my body come alive.

"Why'd you c-call me that earlier?" I asked, my voice slightly muffled. Even the cold couldn't get what he'd said out of my mind.

"Call you what?"

"Your girl."

The rise and fall of his chest froze for a second before he nuzzled me closer. "I don't know, Oak." His words were softer than I'd ever heard them before. "Try to get some sleep."

I let it go, allowing the exhaustion to take over. This was so wrong, but no part of me wanted to do the right thing and ask him to take me home.

Right now, I didn't want to be anywhere else but in Lennon's house, cuddled up with him in his bed, using his body to warm me up.

17

LENNON

I'd slept maybe four hours and spent the rest of the night listening to the sound of Oakley breathing as she slept in my arms. Normally, I would have occupied myself with something rather than laying there unable to sleep, but all I wanted to do was feel Oakley warm against my body.

She'd been too cold, barely dressed for fall, let alone winter and freezing temperatures. Her socks were so wet and cold in my hands, I'd half expected her toes to be black when I pulled her socks off. Thankfully, they weren't, but they were so cold she could barely move them.

When she'd asked about my slip-up of calling her my girl, my heart had nearly frozen to death right along with her. I hadn't even realized it slid off my tongue in that moment, but my entire body and mind were screaming to help her, and that guy was in my way.

Instead of choosing to look further into why I'd said it, I slid out from the bed, careful not to wake her as I pulled on my gray sweatpants. As promised, I left a second pair folded up on the end of the bed for when she woke, along with one of my sweatshirts in case she wanted it.

To wear it.

Not to keep it, of course.

Though I wouldn't argue if she did.

God, what was wrong with me?

Frustrated with myself, I grabbed her wet jeans off the ground and headed to the kitchen to make her breakfast, tossing her pants in the dryer on my way. We were both scheduled to work today, but she needed rest, so I pulled out my phone to shoot Jacey and Leo a text.

> **Lennon:** Need you to come in today and open the store. I'll be there when I can.

I set my phone on the black granite countertop and pulled out a pan to set it on the stove top. My kitchen was my favorite place in this house, with its dark counters and white cabinets, to its stainless steel appliances and oak floors. The house was on its last leg when I bought it seven years ago, but I remodeled it. It was the perfect distance to the feed store and my parents' ranch, so I couldn't pass up the opportunity when it hit the market.

My phone buzzed on the counter as I was in the fridge grabbing eggs, cheese, spinach, mushrooms, and sausage. Setting the ingredients beside the stove, I checked my texts.

> **Jacey:** Late night? ;)

> **Lennon:** You going in or not?

> **Jacey:** Yes, boss. Drink some coffee, you're grumpy when you're non-caffeinated.

> **Lennon:** I'm pretty sure it's uncaffeinated.

> **Jacey:** Make that two cups of coffee, please.

I sent back a middle finger emoji and saw that Leo had sent me back a thumbs up. Setting the phone down, getting to work cracking the eggs in the pan, mixing the other ingredients in as the pan heated up. My phone buzzed again, causing me to glance at the screen.

> **Jacey:** Since when does Lennon Bronson send emojis?

I ignored the text and moved to the coffee pot as the eggs cooked. Placing some ground coffee beans in the filter, I clicked a few buttons and let the machine do the rest. As soon as the coffee started coming out, the scent filled my house, along with the scramble cooking on the stove.

From down the hall, I heard my bedroom door squeak open, then click shut, followed by tiny footsteps padding down the hall. Oakley appeared around the corner, rubbing her eyes and looking like the sunrise on the first day of spring.

Her amber hair was mussed up from sleep and my sweats were way too big for her petite form, but even wearing my baggy clothes, she was beautiful.

I forced my eyes off of her before she could see me gawking and brought my attention back to the pan. "Hungry?" I asked.

She was quiet, so I glanced over my shoulder to see her eyes on my bare back.

I probably should have put a shirt on, now that I thought about it.

She was my employee, not some girlfriend I had over for the night. I shouldn't be standing in my kitchen shirtless, making her breakfast and coffee.

She caught me watching her and blinked, averting her gaze. "You don't have to make me breakfast, too. You already went above and beyond letting me stay here and take advantage of your heater," she said, her voice hoarse from sleep.

"I wasn't about to let you sleep in that freezing house, Oak." I turned around to find her slipping onto the barstool at my kitchen island. "You need to run your heater."

Those green eyes bored up at me from where she sat, and I wanted to hug her, wrap my arms around her just to make that look disappear off her face. She looked sad, like she was alone and had no one else to rely on but herself.

"I will. I'm not used to the cold sneaking up so quickly, but I'll run it. I promise."

"It does that out here." I pulled two plates out of the upper cabinet and dished up even portions of the scramble, then poured two cups of coffee.

"I mean, it did in Colorado, too, but I never had to deal with a cold house, so I guess I just wasn't expecting it."

I set a plate and mug in front of her, but remained standing on the opposite side of the island. "What made you leave Colorado?" I asked before taking a bite.

Her fork was halfway to her mouth when she paused. "What?"

I finished swallowing, taking a sip of coffee. "Colorado. Why'd you leave?"

She dropped the bite she was about to take off her fork, then poked at a piece of mushroom with it. "Family."

I waited for her to say more, but she didn't. She finally took a bite, her eyes closing at the taste of the food. After she was done chewing, her eyes found mine. "This is delicious. Thank you."

I nodded, and we ate the rest in silence. Once she was done, I picked up her plate and brought it to the sink. "More coffee?" I asked as I filled my own cup. Turns out, Jacey was getting her way and I was drinking two cups of coffee after all.

"Please, thank you," she said.

I poured the rich liquid into her mug and set the decanter back on the machine.

"Where'd that guy go that was there last night?" she asked after taking a sip.

Setting my mug on the counter, I leaned back against the edge by the sink, crossing my arms. "He left."

"Oh." The look on her face gave no indication on whether she remembered what I'd said to him.

"Do you know him?" I asked.

"Not really. I mean, I've seen him at the store, but that's it." She grabbed her coffee mug and brought it to her lips, the cuffs of my sweatshirt covering her hands to her palms, so only her fingertips were showing.

I nodded, then turned to wash the dishes I'd used for breakfast. "I'm taking you to the rental car place today."

"I need to call a tow truck for my car. I can't leave it there," she said.

"Already done."

"What?" she asked, her voice a slightly higher pitch.

"I already called the tow company."

"When?"

"I slipped out of bed last night to let them know where your car was. They already picked it up and it's in the shop." It was the only reason I'd let myself leave her side all night. My friend Wyatt had no problem taking the car in to fix it.

"At a shop? Lennon, I can't afford a mechanic right now."

I set the dishes on the drying rack after shutting off the water and turned to face her. "What was your plan, Oak? Walk to work in this weather? You don't even have snow boots."

"Yes, I do. They're just in Denver." Her face scrunched as she realized those boots would be no use to her here. "I don't have a plan yet, but I can't just fork up money I don't have."

"It's covered," I stated.

Her green eyes blazed. "I'm not taking your money."

"Not mine. The mechanic is a friend. He's doing the work for free."

"For free?" she squeaked.

I nodded. "Yep. It's also the same mechanic I suggested you take your car to when you rear-ended me, but he said he's never seen the vehicle before."

She opened her mouth but then closed it before she said anything, pursing her lips tight.

"If you don't take care of the car, it's not going to keep running, Oak," I pointed out.

"I know. I was going to take it, but I just-" She stopped, inhaling a deep breath. "You know what? It doesn't matter."

She was frustrated with the whole thing, and I didn't blame her. The entire situation was fucked.

"I'm scheduled today, so I can't go to the rental place until tonight," she said, like it just dawned on her that she had a job. With the events that took place in the last twelve hours, her mind was probably scattered. No car, no money, no heater at home, being in her boss's house, sleeping in her boss's bed. The list could go on and on.

"Jacey's covering your shift. You need to rest and get your heater going in your house. We can stop by there on the way to the rental car place."

"I can't call out of work, Lennon. I just started working there."

I frowned. I was her fucking boss.

"Then consider this me giving you the day off."

She mirrored my frown. "But then Jacey will only have one day off."

I shrugged. "Nothing she isn't used to."

"She'll hate me."

I scoffed, turning around to rinse out my coffee mug and place it in the dishwasher. "Jacey doesn't hate anyone."

Oakley sighed behind me.

"Ready to go?" I asked as I closed the dishwasher and turned to face her.

"My jeans-"

"Are in the dryer. You can keep the sweatshirt. That denim jacket doesn't do shit against the cold."

Fucking hell, Lennon. Keep the sweatshirt? Really?

"I already have one of your coats at home," she stated.

I shrugged. "Keep 'em both."

Her eyes narrowed, then she stood, aiming for the hallway. She paused, not turning to me. "Where's the dryer?"

"Laundry room is the second door on the right," I said, a smile pulling at my mouth.

Her legs started moving again, her tiny hands holding up my sweatpants as she went.

I released a long breath, shaking my head.

I was in for it.

***

"Heater's on," Oakley said. She got in my truck and shoved the coat I'd given her after that night at the bar into my hands.

"I said you can keep it," I grumbled as I shoved the coat off of me and onto the middle seat between us.

Her seat belt clicked into place. "I don't need all your clothes in my closet like you live with me or something."

I raised an eyebrow as I pulled back onto the road and headed for the rental place.

She saw the movement and crossed her arms.

She was still wearing my sweatshirt.

The corner of my lips threatened to tilt up at her in my clothes, but I forced the smile away.

About thirty-five minutes later, we were pulling into the rental building. Bell Buckle was too small of a town to bother with a car rental business, so I had to take her to the one in the next town over.

Thankfully, it wasn't snowing yet, but the snow from last night still stuck to the ground at a height of about six inches. The roads were plowed, but still sludgey.

I shifted my truck into park and opened my door. Before I could make it to her side, she was already out and heading inside the front doors. Sighing, I followed behind her, coming up beside her at the front desk. The lobby had a small waiting room to our left that contained all of four chairs and a small TV that looked like it was from the nineties. The smell of lemon Lysol hung in the air, and the drooping plant in the corner looked like it was suffering from it.

"What can I do for you two today?" the receptionist asked, her brunette ponytail caught in the top of her plaid scarf.

I opened my mouth to reply, but Oakley beat me to it. "I need a rental for a few days."

"All-wheel-drive. Snow tires, and I want chains in the trunk just in case," I demanded.

The woman eyed the two of us, then slowly looked back down at her computer. She clicked her mouse a few times, squinting at the screen. "I have a Toyota Rav4. Not sure what condition the tires are in, and you'll have to supply your own chains if you'd like them. But I can assure you, their all-wheel-drive capability is one of the best in its-"

"I'll buy you chains," I said to Oakley, not bothering to look at her.

I felt her gaze on the side of my face as she glared at me. "We'll take it," I told the receptionist.

"Perfect. Will you both be drivers on the vehicle?" she asked.

Oakley turned back to the woman. "No. Just me."

I crossed my arms, resisting the urge to adjust my hat as Oakley handed the woman her driver's license and insurance card. She typed the information into the computer and then handed them back to Oakley, along with a pen and paper full of information written in tiny script.

"This is the contract for the rental. You can keep it a maximum of fourteen days, and if you need it longer than that, we ask that you call or come in for an extension." She highlighted a line for Oakley to sign.

"I'm hoping I only need it a day or two," Oakley said as she scanned the paper in front of her, then signed her first and last name.

The receptionist offered her an apologetic look as she pulled the paper back and made a copy of it. She swiveled in her chair to grab a set of keys off the hook from the board behind her, then stood, grabbing her coat from the back of her chair and putting it on. She walked around the desk as her hands fumbled to get her ponytail out of the jacket.

"Car's out back," she said as she opened the door to the right of her desk, gesturing for us to go through first.

I grabbed the door, letting Oakley walk through. "Go ahead," I said to the receptionist.

She gave a small smile and walked through. I followed the two of them out as they headed toward the silver Toyota parked in the corner of the lot. The woman unlocked the car, then got in, taking note of the mileage and fuel tank.

"If you could just fill the tank before returning it, please. Otherwise we'll have to charge eight dollars a gallon to fill it here," she stated.

Eight dollars a gallon? Fuck that.

"We'll fill it. Thank you," I told her.

"*I'll* fill it. I appreciate it, ma'am," Oakley said, sending a glare my way.

"Of course. Just remember," she pulled a folded paper from her coat pocket, handing it to Oakley along with the keys, "it's thirty-six dollars a day. This is your copy of the contract. You can pay once you return the vehicle. And don't forget there's a one hundred and fifty dollar cleaning fee as well, if it doesn't come back clean."

Oakley looked like she was about to be sick with the knowledge of how pricey renting this vehicle could be, but she quickly cleared the nausea from her face and shook the woman's hand.

"Thank you again," Oakley said.

The woman pulled her scarf closer to her jaw, warding off the cold. "Of course. Drive safely."

I nodded at her as she retreated back into the building, then I went around the car, checking each tire to ensure they all had tread.

"What are you doing?" Oakley asked as I came around the front of the vehicle.

"Checking the tires. They should do for now, but I'm still getting you chains."

She shook her head, shoving her hands in the front pocket of my hoodie she was wearing. "It's an all-wheel-drive vehicle. It doesn't need chains."

I took the two steps that were separating us, our chests now mere inches from each other. She tipped her head back, but determination shone in her eyes.

"I don't want another call at six-thirty on a fucking work night that you drove off the road because you didn't take the proper precautions while driving in the snow." I should tone it down, but my worry for her when she called made me sick. The short drive to find her was the worst kind of torture, then to find her standing on the side of the road in the snow, let alone with some stranger? My fists clenched as my chest tightened with the memory.

"I'm *so* sorry that I inconvenienced you, but I didn't ask you to drive me to your house. Nor did I ask you to cuddle me all night!" Her voice raised as she pulled her hands free from the pocket with force, sending the keys flying to the snow-covered ground.

I bent to grab them, holding them between our too-close bodies. "I didn't have a choice when you were practically freezing to fucking death."

She grabbed the keys from my hand, her fingertips grazing my palm. "Sorry for fucking calling you," she muttered as she stormed past me toward the driver's side door.

My hand wrapped around her forearm, stopping her before she could get to the door. "I'll be the first person you call if something like that happens again, got it?"

Her eyes were practically throwing green flames at me with the emotions battling inside of her right now. "Why the hell would I do that? You've made it perfectly clear that I ruined your night. Did I interrupt something between you and some girl? Is that why you're so mad?"

"I haven't thought of any other woman since the night you slammed into the back of my truck. So no, you didn't interrupt me getting off with some girl. And you're going to call me because I fucking said so."

She ripped her arm from my hand, which wasn't too hard as I barely had any grip on her. "You can boss me around at work, Lennon, but not out here. I'm not just your employee. I'm a person, too."

I dropped my hand to my side, searching her eyes. "No, you're not," I said quietly. She wasn't just my employee, and my mind was starting to realize that.

"What?"

I shook my head as I noticed a snowflake land in her hair. The color difference was astronomical. Oakley was all fire with her amber hair, rosy cheeks, and flaming eyes. Somehow, she looked even more beautiful with that snowflake against the red strands.

"Do you need a driving lesson?" I asked, my voice softer now.

"What?" she squeaked again, taken back slightly by the change in my tone.

"Do you need me to teach you how to drive in the snow?"

She blinked, shaking her head like she was trying to comprehend what I was saying. I didn't want to keep going at it with her. There was no reason to. She was stressed, and igniting the flame with my concern for her wellbeing wasn't going to make things better right now. It didn't make any sense to her, and it sure as hell didn't make any sense to me.

"I grew up in Denver," she replied, like that was answer enough.

"City streets are different than out here, and you've got a long stretch of freeway to get back."

"I'll be fine. Plus, I'm sure you'll stick to my ass the whole way anyway."

I shrugged, opening the driver's side door for her. Anger was still prevalent on her face as she slid behind the wheel and punched the button to start the car.

"Drive safe," I clipped before closing the door and walking around the building to my truck parked out front. I slid in to find my jacket Oakley had left on the middle seat.

God, I was an idiot.

18

Lennon

I'd followed her all the way home. Even though her house was out of the way for getting to the feed store, I wanted to make sure she got home safe and didn't slide off into another ditch.

The rental car cut through the snow no problem, and by the time I had made it to work, the snow was coming down in thick sheets of white.

After a long day at work, I clicked on my blinker, my windshield wipers doing their best to keep my view clear, and turned onto Callan's road. He lived a few minutes from Bottom of the Buckle Ranch, but I wasn't up for seeing everyone tonight, so I'd asked him if we could hang out at his place. I didn't want to go home and wash the sweats Oakley wore or make the bed she slept in.

I ran a hand over my mouth, frustrated with myself at the effect Oakley was having on me.

Shifting the truck into park, I got out with my six-pack of beer and climbed the porch steps, letting myself in. Callan's house was a small, white farmhouse on a couple acres with a wrap-around porch and a porch swing. It was a three-bed, two-bath house, but he was the only one who lived here. He taught kids how to ride horses for a living, and it made me wonder why he hadn't started a family of his own since he loved kids so much.

I found Callan on the couch watching the rodeo that was being streamed on TV.

"Beckham on there?" I asked as I set the six-pack in the fridge and grabbed two for me and Callan, uncapping them and tossing the bottle caps in the trash.

"He's next," Callan said when I sat down on the couch, handing him his beer.

He took it and tossed his head back, taking a long pull.

"Long day?" I asked.

He leaned back, draping his arm over the back of the couch with his beer propped on his knee. "No."

Callan always got nervous watching our brother Beckham ride broncs. Callan had a big heart, and seeing someone he loved put himself in danger for fun always made him anxious.

The camera moved to Beck propped up on the chute about to get on the back of a bronc while the announcer's voice boomed over the TV, announcing where he was from and how many points he'd accumulated throughout the season. This was Beck's last show before he got to come home for the winter, and we were all eager to see him for this longer length of time instead of just the usual few days here and there during the season.

Out of the corner of my eye, I saw Callan shaking his head the slightest bit. He always supported Beck, but that didn't mean he had to like what he did.

On the TV, Beckham mounted the clearly agitated gelding and adjusted his hand on the rope. Once he was situated, he nodded once, and the gate flew open. The horse took off, angry as all hell. He bucked like no other, doing everything he could to get Beck off of him, but Beck held strong, rocking back and forth with the momentum rather than fighting it.

Too long later, the eight-second timer buzzed, and the two pickup men rushed to get Beck off the bronc. He'd score high with how mean that horse was, which I'm sure he was thrilled about guessing by the big smile on his face.

Beck looped an arm around the waist of one of the men and swung off. Callan clicked off the TV before they could announce his points, clearly only watching it to see that Beck was okay.

"What about you?" he asked, returning to our previous conversation before Beckham came out.

"Long doesn't even begin to describe it." I took a swig of beer, wishing it was something stronger.

"Oakley okay? You never updated us on how she was." I'd forgotten I'd left Reed's house in a hurry after she'd called, giving them minimal details about why I was leaving.

"She is now. Any longer and she probably would've got frostbite. Her car's in the shop with Wyatt."

"Any idea what's wrong with it?" he asked.

"Not sure. It could've been from sliding off the road, or when she hit me."

His eyes widened. "She hit you?"

Shit.

I scratched the back of my neck under the bill of my cap. I thought about the way Oakley's eyes always heated when my hat was backwards and my lips twitched.

"She rear-ended me the night before her interview."

"That girl's got a bad track record with driving, it seems," he observed.

That was the understatement of the century. I was surprised Oakley made it from Denver to Bell Buckle in one piece.

"I just feel bad for how I treated her at the rental place. I was so damn scared she was hurt, Cal." I leaned forward, resting my elbows on my knees.

"I know the feeling. The not-so-fun perks of caring about someone. But if you feel bad, just apologize to her."

I looked over my shoulder at him where he sat on the other end of the couch. "That easy?"

He nodded. "Girls love when you take ownership of the shit you did wrong."

I scoffed, hanging my head. "Says the guy who hasn't been in a relationship in years."

He picked at the label on his beer. "I'm just focusing on my career."

"You sound like me," I muttered.

"But seriously, invite her over to Mom and Dad's or something."

I looked over my shoulder at him. "Tomorrow night?" My parents always had monthly dinners for us all to get together and catch up. Family was a big thing to them.

"Yeah, I'm sure she'd love a home-cooked meal, and she knows everyone. Well, besides Mom and Dad."

Oakley *had* seemed to be living off of noodles, so his statement about the food was true. "But should her boss really be asking her to his family's home?" I asked him, leaning back against the couch.

He shrugged. "She called you when she was on the side of the road, didn't she?"

"Yeah, but that was because I was the only number she had to call aside from Lettie."

He sat forward. "You're thinking too much into this, Len. Just ask her, and the worst she can say is no."

I took another sip of my beer, already thinking of how I could ask her without coming off as creepy. I mean, she had already slept in my bed. What was wrong with a family dinner?

***

BEAT AROUND THE BUSH

I'd avoided Oakley at all costs during my shift, but not because I didn't want to see her. I still felt like a dick for the way I'd behaved at the rental place, like I had some right to be that protective over her.

She could hold her own, and she didn't need me coming in like some alpha male trying to boss her around.

Even though I *was* her boss.

At work, it was getting harder and harder to remember that she was my employee, and today was proof of that. Anytime she walked by my office or called for backup at the front, I couldn't stop myself from thinking of her legs tangled with mine in my bed. But shortly after, I'd remember the way I acted yesterday and hate myself for it.

I'd finished counting the money from the register and was bending to lock it in the safe when Oakley walked by my office, most likely on her way to clock out.

Ensuring the safe was locked, I stood and grabbed my coat, then headed for the break room to find her trying to type her pin into the screen. It kept flashing a denied code at her, and she cursed under her breath.

I came up behind her and reached over her shoulder to override the code as she froze, then I gestured for her to try again. "Sometimes it's finicky."

She tapped at the numbers and it accepted her clock out time. "I'll say," she muttered.

She turned, but I hadn't given her much space, so she came face to face with my chest. She angled her head up, a skeptical look in her eyes. "You here to lecture me some more?"

I sighed, taking one step back to give her some room. "No," I admitted, bringing my hand up to scratch at the back of my neck. "I actually wanted to apologize for how I acted yesterday."

She raised an eyebrow, crossing her arms. "Really?" By the tone of her voice, she didn't sound very convinced.

"Yeah, I was out of line, and I'm sorry for treating you like you can't hold your own."

"How do you know I can?" she asked.

I crossed my arms, mirroring her. "You drove to the middle of nowhere without a plan, you found a job within days of arriving, and you don't ask anyone for anything."

She scoffed. "I wouldn't say not asking people for help is a trait to be admired."

I shrugged. "I say it is. Does it make you stubborn? Yeah. But at least you know you're strong enough to figure shit out on your own."

Her eyes narrowed. "I thought this was an apology."

I winced. I guess I did just call her stubborn. "Do I need to get on my knees and beg? Would that make you feel better?"

She shrugged, looking around the room with cool indifference. "I suppose that could help persuade me to accept your apology."

I heaved a sigh, accepting that this was the way it had to go. I dropped to my knees, looking up at her. Her eyes shot to me, wide with shock. "I didn't actually mean-"

"Oakley, please forgive me for the way I acted yesterday and come to dinner at my parents' house tonight."

If only Callan knew this was how the apology would go.

She looked like she was contemplating my offer, but she couldn't seem to hold back the smile on her face as she stared down at me before her. God, I was so close to her, so close to a place her boss should never be. It took all I had in me not to glance at her thighs and what was between them.

"Hmm. I don't know." She hummed, contemplating accepting my apology. She brought a finger up, tapping her lower lip.

She was dragging this out on purpose, which meant she liked me kneeling before her.

The thought had my cock hardening in my jeans.

"Do I need to be a little more persuasive?" I asked.

Her eyes casually studied me before her. "Depends what that includes."

I smirked. "It wouldn't include talking."

Her eyes widened slightly before she cleared her throat. "I'll go. But it's not a date, just so we're clear," she said.

I nodded. I didn't care what she labeled it as. I just wanted to spend more time around her.

She pursed her lips, then rolled her eyes. "You can get up now, you know. In case I wasn't clear, I accept your apology."

I stood, towering over her again. I wasn't sure if I liked this angle more, or being down on the ground before her.

"I'll pick you up at eight so you can get ready."

I walked her to her rental car after locking up, then parted ways with her and headed for my truck. Unable to help the buzz of anticipation of seeing her again tonight, I smiled like an idiot all the way home.

19

OAKLEY

It took no time at all to get home with the roads plowed and the rental eating up the slushy streets like it was a sunny day in June.

I had no idea what to wear to Lennon's family dinner tonight. Given my limited wardrobe at the moment, I didn't have many options to choose from. I laid out a white wool turtleneck sweater and my light wash jeans, then headed for the shower to wash the smell of the feed store off of me.

After I toweled off, I slipped on my clothes and decided to put on a little bit of the makeup that I'd found in the center console of my Subaru when I first got here and was unloading my belongings.

I put on a bit of concealer and mascara, deciding to skip on the blush since my cheeks did a good job of staining red by themselves. Since I didn't have any lip gloss, I opted for a bit of Vaseline. It was always better than chapstick anyway.

After I fixed my hair in the mirror for the third time, I stopped myself. Why was I overthinking how I looked for Lennon and his family? It wasn't like we were dating, and I had no obligation to impress them.

Yet, a big part of me wanted them to like me. I'd already met his siblings, but I wanted his parents to like me too. As much as I shouldn't, I cared what people thought of me, so I pegged my desire to be liked by his family off on my people pleasing problems.

I would've said no, but how was I supposed to reject him when he was quite literally on his knees begging? His apology was unexpected, but I never once would have thought he was going to invite me to his parents' house. It all took me by surprise, and I had seconds to make my decision.

Hopefully I made the right one.

A knock sounded at the front door and I grabbed my purse and denim jacket, rushing out of my room to look out the peephole. Lennon was standing there like some sort of gentleman picking me up for a date.

Not a date, Oakley.

Ugh, couldn't he have just honked his horn or something?

Opening the door, I pasted on my best I'm-not-overthinking-this smile. "Hello."

"Hey, Oak. Ready?" Lennon asked. He was wearing a Carhartt brown jacket with his typical jeans and cowboy boots. Thankfully for my sake, his hat was facing forward.

"Yep." I stepped over the threshold, closing and locking the door behind me. I turned and found myself too close to him on my tiny porch.

He was looking down at me like he had something to say, but kept his mouth shut and turned on the heel of his boot to head for his truck.

I followed, getting in on the passenger side after he opened the door for me. He closed it, coming around to his side to get in. The truck was still running with the heat on, so he shifted into drive and headed down my street.

"You look nice," he said quietly, keeping his gaze on the road.

"Thanks. You do, too." Looking down at my sweater, I felt a little overdressed compared to him.

You're overthinking it. It's just a sweater, not some ball gown.

The ride to his parents' ranch was silent, until I blurted out, "What if they don't like me?"

We passed under the arch to their house as he smiled, adjusting his grip on the wheel with the bumpiness of the dirt - well, now more like mud due to the snow - road. "My mom loves everyone."

"And your dad?"

He glanced at me, shifting the truck into park in front of the large white farmhouse. "He's a grump, but nothing to be scared of."

I stared up at the house before me, a coating of snow on the roof with warm lights illuminating the area around the home. The property, from what I could see, was huge. The moon reflected off the snow covered land that stretched for miles before us. There were three barns that were each a different size, a covered arena, an outdoor arena, pastures, trailers, trucks - basically everything you could think of on a ranch, was here.

This was where Lennon grew up?

"Why are you nervous they won't like you?" he asked, interrupting my gawking.

I turned to face him in my seat, not sure how to answer that. Why *would* his employee be nervous they wouldn't like her? Shouldn't it not matter?

"I just don't want them to convince you to fire me or something." I stumbled over the words, spitting out the first thing that came to mind.

He killed the engine. "No one can convince me to do anything I don't want to do. Come on."

I guess he went down willingly when he got on his knees for me earlier, then.

He got out and came around the hood of the truck as my fingers twisted in the sleeves of my sweater. Opening the door, he took a step back to allow me room to step out.

Sliding off the seat, I looked down at my sneakers, the toes digging into the mud from where they'd plowed the driveway. The door closed behind me, and Lennon passed me, making his way up the porch steps. I followed, trying to push away the nerves eating at me.

I'd never been to a guy's parents' house before, let alone my boss's. I'd met Lennon's siblings at the bar, but that didn't make it any less nerve-wracking. It was one thing to hang out with someone at a bar, but in their home? It felt way more intimate.

He held the front door open for me, and I stepped in, waiting for him to lead the way.

The house was warm and open, instantly giving the cozy feeling that most childhood homes emitted. The smell of warm food wafted from the kitchen as we stepped out of the front entry to the bustle of people hanging around the living room and dining area.

"Len!" Lettie said from the kitchen, setting down her glass of wine to come over to hug her brother. She let him go, then pulled me in for a hug. "It's so nice to see you." She let me go, a huge grin on her face. "I hope my brother hasn't been playing the mean manager role on you."

I smiled, shaking my head. "He's been great."

From the kitchen, I heard another familiar voice. "Come on, Lettie. Lennon ain't the mean one. That's Reed." Callan grinned from where he was stirring something in a bowl.

Brandy was setting the table with plates as she scoffed. "He's not just mean."

Sitting on the couch, Reed said over his shoulder without looking back, "What else am I, Brandy?"

She rolled her eyes, ignoring him.

"That's what I thought," Reed muttered.

Lettie clapped her hands together. "My mom's in her room, but I'll go get her."

I reached out to grab her arm. "No, you really don't have-" I shut my mouth. It was too late.

Lettie disappeared down the hall and I cringed. Great first impression if people are pulling Mrs. Bronson away from what she's doing to come greet me.

I slipped out of my jacket, noticing that Lennon had shed his sometime between us walking in the door and now. He took mine from me without asking, hanging it on the hook by the door.

"You want something to drink? Wine? Beer?" he asked, turning back to me.

"Water's fine. Thank you." I'd feel bad drinking their alcohol since I didn't bring anything for them.

Fuck, I didn't bring anything for his mom.

Lennon disappeared into the kitchen and I came up next to Brandy at the dining table. "Do you need help with anything?" I asked her.

Brandy shook her head. "Don't even think about helping, Oakley. You're our guest. Make yourself comfortable."

Lennon came back with a glass of wine, holding it out to me. "But I wanted-"

"Just take it, Oak," he grumbled. "Water's in the fridge if you want it that bad."

I bit back my retort as his mom came around the corner. Recognition hit me in the chest. I'd already met her before. Well, *seen* her before. She was at the booth when Lettie recommended that I apply to Tumbleweed Feed.

"It's so nice to see you again, Oakley," Mrs. Bronson said as she wrapped me in a hug.

"You, too," I replied, my voice muffled against her shoulder.

"Again?" Lennon questioned.

She pulled back, looking up at Lennon. "I was at the fundraising event when she came by our booth for Bottom of the Buckle."

Lennon looked at me like I was supposed to know I'd met her before, and I shrugged. How was I supposed to connect the dots? At the time, I didn't even know she was Lettie's mother.

"Make yourself at home, sweetheart. Dinner's almost ready," she said with a sweet smile.

"Thank you, Mrs. Bronson."

"Please, call me Charlotte." She turned, then disappeared into the kitchen to help Callan with whatever he was doing.

The front door opened, letting in a burst of cold air. Boots stomped, and an indiscernible low mumble came from the front entry. An older man with a graying mustache stepped into the room, a scowl on his face. "Damn cows always-"

"Dad, this is Oakley. My new employee," Lennon introduced me, cutting his father off.

Mr. Bronson looked at me from under the brim of a creme-colored wool cowboy hat. He pulled his glove off his right hand, holding it out to me. "Nice to meet you, Oakley. I'm Travis."

I shook it, noting that Lennon watched the movement. "Nice to meet you too, Mr. Bronson. You have a lovely home."

He let go, waving me off. "That's all thanks to Charlotte. She keeps the house pretty, I keep the ranch pretty."

I smiled. "Didn't know a ranch could be kept pretty, with all the chaos going on and such."

He took his hat off, hanging it on the hook with his coat. "Now this girl knows what's going on. She's a keeper." He shot a wink to Lennon.

Lennon sighed. "She's my employee, Dad. Not my girlfriend."

"That why she's standing in my house?" he asked as he walked by, heading down the hallway.

My cheeks flushed at his dad pointing out the obvious. Why *was* I in Lennon's parents' home? A simple apology would have sufficed. But yet, here I was, standing in Travis and Charlotte's home, surrounded by their family.

The front door behind me opened again, and I turned to find Bailey walking through the door with a pie in his hands. "Sorry I'm late. Those damn cows-"

"Baby!" Lettie squealed, and Lennon rolled his eyes.

Bailey's expression softened as she threw her arms around his neck, the pie balanced in one hand. I took it from him to save it from ending up on the floor.

"Hey, Huckleberry," he murmured to her as I brought the pie to the kitchen.

"How's it going, Oakley? Or I guess I should be asking how your car is," Callan asked as he rinsed lettuce for a salad, a smirk pulling at the corner of his lips.

"What happened to her car?" Brandy asked from where she stood getting utensils out of the drawer.

"She drove into a ditch," Lennon said at the same time Callan said, "She hit Lennon's truck."

"She hit Lennon's truck?" Lettie asked from behind me.

I winced. Lennon's eyes landed on me after he shot Callan a glare.

"When did this happen?" Charlotte asked.

"The night before my interview at the feed store," I replied.

Reed inhaled a sharp breath of air. "Damn."

Lennon shot a glare at him, too. "Both our vehicles are fine. We're fine. Let's just let it go."

"Isn't her car in the shop?" Callan asked innocently, yet Lennon and I both knew he was stirring the pot.

"You don't have a car right now?" Lettie asked.

I turned to face her. "I do, it's just being worked on."

"Oakley didn't put your old truck out of commission yet?" Reed asked Lennon.

"Sounds like the beginning of a love story to me," Travis muttered as he came back into the room, passing between me and Lennon to grab a beer from the fridge.

"Let's get some air," Lennon said hurriedly, grabbing my hand and leading me out to the back porch and sliding the door shut behind us.

As soon as we were outside, he dropped my hand, taking his hat off and running his hand through his hair. "Sorry about them."

I stuck to my spot by the door, watching him place his hat back on. "It's okay."

He scoffed. "It's not. They're being asses."

"I'm used to asshole families, and when I tell you they're not, I mean it."

He looked down at me, his brow furrowed. Right when I thought he was about to press further, he said, "We can leave if you want."

"I want to stay."

He looked slightly taken aback. "You do?"

I nodded. "Yeah. I like them. Plus, it beats sitting at home alone."

He looked back and forth between my eyes like he was trying to see if I was lying or not. He must've found the answer he was looking for, because he nodded, then said, "Yeah, okay. Let's go back inside, then. It's cold out here."

***

"It was really nice seeing you, Oakley. Don't be a stranger," Charlotte said into my hair as she hugged me goodbye.

"You, too, Charlotte." But I couldn't make any promises about the stranger part.

She disappeared into the kitchen to help Callan and Reed with the cleanup from dinner. Travis had retired to bed early after grumbling something about having to be up at the crack of dawn.

I slipped on my coat as Lettie wrapped her scarf around her neck, then pulled her gloves on. "The poor single guys have to help with cleanup duty."

Lennon frowned, fixing the collar on his coat. "I'm single, too, Lettie."

She rolled her eyes while Bailey set his felt cowboy hat back on his head. "You should come to the skijoring event tomorrow," Bailey said to me.

"Skijoring?" I had no idea what that was.

"People pull skiers on horseback. They do some small jumps and try to beat each other's times around the track," Lettie answered.

I looked up to find Lennon watching me, waiting for my answer. Bringing my gaze back to Lettie, I said, "Sure. That sounds fun. I just don't know how to ski."

She smiled. "Neither do I, but it's fun to watch. We can drink naughty hot chocolates while they do all the work."

"Sounds like a plan to me," I said.

"You ready to go, Huckleberry?" Bailey asked Lettie. She'd told me during dinner that he called her that because of a prank he pulled that landed her ass in a bucket of huckleberries when they were younger.

She reached up to kiss his cheek. "Yup."

"How 'bout you, Oak?" Lennon asked.

Speaking of nicknames.

Heat crept up my neck for literally no reason at all. He'd called me that probably a dozen times before. "I'm ready."

Lennon held the front door open for us, and Callan shouted his goodbye as we headed out the door. Brandy had left shortly after Travis went to bed for some emergency at her mom's house, so I'd already said my goodbyes to her earlier.

We headed down the porch steps, saying our goodbyes to Bailey and Lettie as they got in Bailey's truck.

Lennon opened the passenger door, giving me space to get in the vehicle.

"You don't have to go if you don't want to. They won't be offended if you say no," he said, still standing with the door open as I buckled myself in.

"I do want to go," I admitted. It was fun hanging out with them, and I liked seeing this side of Lennon. Who he was when he was around family and not just when he was a manager and owner of a retail store.

His brows pulled together. "You do?"

I nodded. "Yeah. It'll be fun."

He looked down at my shoes, a frown pulling at his mouth. He closed my door and came around, starting the engine to get the heat going.

As Lennon drove me back to my house, I stared out the window as we passed snow-covered fields and wondered if I'd said yes not because I wanted to hang out with his siblings, but to get another chance to see Lennon again outside of work.

20

LENNON

Jacey and Leo were holding down the fort at Tumbleweed Feed to allow me to have today off. I rarely had a day out of that place, so I pushed all work-related thoughts to the side. I could stress about the leasing company not emailing me back tomorrow.

Today was a day to have fun and forget about that shit.

My eyes darted to my watch for what had to be the hundredth time at this point. Oakley was supposed to show up fifteen minutes ago, and I was damn close to getting in my truck to go find her and make sure she hadn't driven herself off the road again.

"She's probably fine, Len. Chill out," Bailey said as he handed me a beer.

Probably didn't make me feel any better.

I took the beer in my gloved hand, but didn't take a sip.

"Women give us a run for our money, don't they?" he asked before knocking his drink back.

I raised an eyebrow at him. "Lettie?"

"She's got a mind of her own," he mumbled.

I chuckled, giving in and taking a swig of my beer. "Tell me about it. I grew up in the same house as her."

"I technically did, too, and let me tell you, the woman hasn't changed, but I love her all the more for it," he said through a smile.

"You talking shit?" Lettie asked as she approached, with Brandy by her side, carrying two thermoses in each hand full of what I assumed was naughty hot chocolates.

Bailey grinned at her, his eyes softening with each step she took toward us. The man was head over heels for her. "Never."

She stopped at Bailey's side. She was wearing black snow pants and a puffy brown jacket. "Good. Anyone want one? I made an extra." She held up one of the mugs.

Bailey and I both lifted our beers, showing we already had a drink.

"Where's Oakley?" Brandy asked, looking around at the group prepping the track that the horses would be galloping on soon.

As if the universe heard us, Oakley's rental car came cruising up the driveway, coming to a stop in front of the main house where the snow was plowed out of the way.

The corners of my lips lifted at the sight of her getting out of the car wearing a full-on snow outfit. She looked like a puffy little marshmallow, her pants and coat all white, paired with white snow boots that had fur sticking out the top. She was wearing an ivory beanie that she promptly adjusted lower on her forehead, her red hair billowing over her shoulders, contrasting the light colors of her coat.

I approached her, wearing my jeans and typical carhartt brown jacket. Not to fool anyone into thinking I was too cool for snow gear, though. I had thermals on underneath. I just didn't need all the waterproof clothing given I wasn't skiing today.

"All dressed for the occasion, huh?" I teased as she met me halfway across the driveway.

Oakley rolled her eyes. "Lettie dropped it all off last night. I didn't want to disappoint her by not wearing it. I tried to reject the clothes, but she doesn't really take no for an answer."

I chuckled. "You think you want to try skiing today?" I asked, not sure what her plan was.

Those green eyes stood out amongst everything else as she looked up at me. "I can try, but I promise I'll fall."

I smiled. "Falling's part of the fun. I'll teach you."

Her fair cheeks turned rosy, even the tip of her nose getting some of the color. I wasn't sure if it was from the cold or my offer to teach her how to ski, but either way, I needed to stop looking into it.

She looked behind me at the group of people near the track. Neighbors from all around came by for this every year, but I didn't want her to be nervous that everyone would see her fall.

"We can practice over by the barn," I offered.

Her eyes met mine again. "Whatever works. I'm not picky."

We walked side by side back to Bailey, Lettie, and Brandy as Travis and Reed saddled up the horses by the barn.

Lettie held out one of the mugs for her. "Here you go."

"Naughty hot chocolate?" Oakley asked, remembering from last night.

"They're so good. Let me know if you need more vodka." She pulled a little flask out of her pocket for emphasis.

Oakley took a sip of the warm liquid, the steam billowing around her face as she drank. "It's perfect. Thanks, Lettie."

"You can always count on me to bring the alcohol," Lettie said with a wink.

"You ready to practice or do you want to finish your drink first?" I asked Oakley.

She licked the chocolate liquid off her top lip before saying, "I can drink and ski at the same time."

"Is that considered drinking and driving?" Brandy asked.

Lettie narrowed her eyes in thought. "Hmm, I'm not sure. I mean, they can pull you over on a horse, so I'd assume the same goes for skiing."

"Still think that shit's ridiculous," Bailey announced. "Getting pulled over on a horse for drinking? I mean, come on."

Their voices drowned out as they went on about all the moving things you could get a DUI on while I turned to Oakley. "You sure about drinking and skiing? With your driving record, I'm not sure that's a great idea," I teased.

She glared up at me, taking another long sip of her drink. "I'm a great driver," she insisted.

I couldn't help but smile at that.

"What?" she squeaked. "It was two times."

"Since you've been in Bell Buckle."

Her jaw dropped and I chuckled.

I held my hands up in mock surrender. "Alright, I'll stop. Just make sure you concentrate on your balance and not my hands on you, and you'll be fine."

Her cheeks turned a deeper shade of red, but this time, I knew it wasn't because of the cold.

***

"How does anyone do this?" Oakley complained after falling for the sixth time.

"It's all in how you balance, which I'm now seeing you don't have much of," I said, lending her a hand to help her up.

"The snow is so damn slippery," she stated as she wiped her gloved hands on her pants. "There's no way people slide over that gracefully."

I snorted. "Didn't you grow up in Colorado? That's like the world's biggest playground for skiers."

She reached around to wipe the snow off her ass. "That doesn't mean I'm good at it."

"Clearly," I mumbled.

She whacked my arm with her gloved hand, the hit soft. I chuckled, then regained my composure. "Come on, let's try again. Just keep your hand in mine this time."

"I can't hold your hand forever," she pointed out.

I shrugged. "What would be the problem with that?"

I froze at the same time she did.

I should not have said that.

After a few seconds of silence, I cleared my throat, holding my hand out to her. "Can't learn if you don't practice."

Her hand fit perfectly in mine, and I wished we didn't have our gloves in the way.

"After today, I think I'm done with this practice stuff."

"Going pro?" I teased.

She shot me a glare out of the side of her eye as I walked alongside her, pulling her slightly to give her momentum. She practiced moving her skis in and out of a triangle shape like I told her to.

She did great every time, until I let her go. Then she'd overthink it, lose her balance, and fall on her ass.

After about twenty feet of holding onto her, she nodded. "Okay, I think I'm ready."

"You sure this time?"

"Yes, I'm sure. Let go," she demanded, determined to keep her balance.

I didn't want to let go of her.

But I did.

She moved her skis, gaining a little bit of speed on the tiny hill I'd gotten her over to. "I'm doing it!" she screamed back to me.

I smiled, watching her red hair blow slightly in the cool breeze. "Keep going, Oak!" I yelled back.

She made it to the bottom of the tiny hill, throwing her arms up in the air as she kept sliding forward. "I did it, Len!"

"Now stop yourself like I showed you," I shouted to her.

But instead of successfully stopping herself, she half turned, then tumbled over, falling on her side and rolling.

Shit.

I ran down the hill, my boots kicking up snow behind me. I made it to her, her form shaking with what had to be her crying.

"Oak, are you okay?" I asked, crouching down in front of her. "Are you hurt?"

She moved her hair out of her face, looking up at me with the biggest smile on her face. She was *laughing*.

I plucked her beanie from the snow and held it dangling between my knees.

"That was so much fun," she said through her giggles.

I smiled, loving the carefree Oakley that was coming out of her shell.

"You fell," I pointed out.

"I think that was the best part," she admitted.

I raised an eyebrow. "Really?"

"I was going so fast," she said.

I didn't point out that she was moving at practically a snail's pace. I knew what it felt like to fly on skis, and if she felt even remotely close to that going down that bunny hill, I wouldn't rain on her parade.

"You were. You did great, Oak." I reached forward, brushing the snow out of her hair, then pulled the beanie down over her head, adjusting it so the hem sat right above her eyebrows.

"I don't think I'm ready for a horse to pull me, though," she admitted.

My smile widened. "Really? I mean, you're basically a pro now."

She rolled her eyes, placing her hands in the snow to push herself up. "Don't flatter me. I know I still suck."

"Here, let me get the skis off you before you stand up." I pulled her foot out a bit, then worked at the restraints keeping her left foot in. Once that one was unclasped, I got to work on the other.

"Thanks," she said softly as she watched my gloved fingers work.

"Of course," I replied, pulling the skis out of the way. I held a hand out to her to help her up and she grabbed it. Standing up, I pulled her with me.

"Wanna watch some of the horses do their runs before we head inside?" I asked her.

She nodded. "Are you riding at all?"

"Maybe. I haven't decided yet." But if she wanted me to, I would. Knowing she'd be watching me fly around that track had me wanting to do a few laps.

I let go of her hand, despite my desire to keep holding it, and we walked side by side up the tiny hill toward the track. I propped the skis in the snow before we found Bailey, Lettie, and Brandy standing by the track as Reed rode by at a gallop on one of the horses, a skier flying behind him.

The skier behind Reed's horse veered to the left, hitting a slight jump. He landed it perfectly, the horse not once breaking stride as the tension on the rope pulled taut.

They finished their lap, and Reed slowed his horse, walking off the adrenaline from the run.

"You don't want to try it?" Lettie asked Oakley.

Oakley shook her head. "If you saw how terrible my little ski lesson just went, you would not be asking that."

Brandy laughed. "I can't ski for shit either. I have more fun on the horse anyway."

"I'm sure Cal would pull you slow," Lettie said.

"Slow or not, I'd still fall on my ass," Brandy remarked.

Bailey turned to the girls. "And probably break another bone."

Brandy narrowed her eyes at him. "Is anyone going to let that go?"

Lettie shrugged. "I'd call yourself lucky for having worked with horses all your life and you've only broken a finger."

"A horse broke your finger?" Oakley asked.

Brandy held the finger she broke out to her, which was now fully healed. "Technically, a horse's ass broke my finger on a fence panel. What a lame way to get hurt."

I watched as Callan got ready with another skier on the track, the two of them discussing their run. Reed was now over by our parents on his horse, talking to some of the locals by the finish line.

Oakley was engaged in her conversation with Lettie and Brandy as Bailey watched as more horses passed with various skiers behind them. I tried my best to pay attention to the track, but every time Oakley laughed beside me, my mind was pulled to her.

It seemed that was happening a lot lately.

21

OAKLEY

I stood to the side of the track with Brandy and Lettie as Lennon got ready to do a lap on his horse, Winston. He'd decided to do a lap before they began wrapping up for the day, and I was glad for it. Between his cowboy hat and leather chaps, I was a goner. Brandy and Lettie were lost in conversation beside me, but I wasn't paying attention to what they were talking about with all my focus on Lennon as he double-checked the saddle and mounted Winston.

The second his ass hit the saddle, I was awestruck. Lennon Bronson on a horse was an image I wanted to see every day. It was probably inappropriate to be thinking of him this way right now, but I was blaming my thoughts on the cold and the naughty hot chocolates.

The skier got ready behind him, and once he signaled that he was set to go, Lennon's thighs tensed and they took off.

It was like the entire earth shook under Winston's hooves. The air bent to their will as they flew, every atom in the universe standing at attention for Lennon's instruction. Winston was a force to be reckoned with, with his beefy muscles and determined eyes, but Lennon was the manpower behind that horse. He was the leader, and fuck, if that didn't turn me on.

Seeing Lennon whip that horse around the track with nothing but hard determination in his eyes did something to me.

Something I didn't want to go away.

Lennon's face was all stone, his entire mood serious as he and Winston sped through the snow, chunks of white kicking up behind them. The skier maneuvered through the snow with ease, like he was barely breaking a sweat despite Winston pulling him at a full gallop.

In what felt like seconds, they were crossing the finish line. Lennon gently slowed Winston as the skier did the same, angling the tips of his skis together.

"Go over there," Lettie urged me.

"What?" I asked, snapping out of my trance.

"He's not running again, so go over to him," she said.

I dug the toe of my boot in the snow. "I don't know…"

"Girl, go! We all know you want to," Brandy exclaimed.

"Is it that obvious?" I asked.

"Your jaw was practically laying on the snow," Lettie admitted.

Brandy snorted as I blew out a breath. "Fine."

I left the comfort of my spot next to the two of them and headed toward Lennon, who was still atop Winston while talking to Bailey and Travis.

I approached from the side, thankful I at least knew not to approach a horse from behind. Bailey glanced at me, then said something to Lennon. Lennon looked over at me, then said something to the two of them and turned Winston toward me, leading him in my direction.

Once he was a few feet from me, I stopped.

"Having fun?" Lennon asked.

I nodded, glancing at the track where another skier was already being pulled behind another horse. "Lettie and Brandy have been keeping me occupied."

"Skijoring not doing it for you?"

Oh, little did he know.

"I love it."

He smiled. "I'm glad. I'd hate for you to be bored."

With this as my view? Never.

"Are you going around again?" I asked him even though Lettie told me he wasn't.

He shook his head. "Just the once. I was actually going to untack Winston, if you wanted to help me."

"Yeah, of course."

He swung a leg over, dismounting from the horse. He kept the reins in his hand, turning to face me. We were close. Too close. Our breaths were coming out in little clouds, the puffs mingling in the air before dissipating.

"The barn will probably be warmer. There's a space heater in there," he said, his hazel eyes locked on mine.

Cheers erupted behind me, but I didn't turn to look at what they were for. Not with Lennon standing in front of me, his horse behind him.

Who allowed cowboys to even exist? Because this should be illegal.

"Right. The barn." I took a step back, allowing him room to pass.

"Come on." He started walking and I kept pace beside him, glancing back at Winston behind us.

Horses were so fucking massive this close up.

"You enjoying the hot chocolate?" Lennon asked, making small talk.

I nodded as we entered the barn, the temperature instantly warmer in there. "Lettie sure makes them strong."

He chuckled, coming up in front of Winston's stall. He opened the door, leading Winston inside. I leaned against the frame of the door, watching as he slid the bit out of Winston's mouth and looped the bridle over his shoulder. Winston stood perfectly still, waiting for Lennon to do his thing.

"I've never tried one of them," he admitted.

"Why not?"

"Not a huge fan of alcohol and dairy mixed together." He walked around Winston, laying something over the saddle. I knew some of the basics of the tack, but the rest of it escaped me.

Maybe one day he could teach me what all of it was and what purpose each piece of equipment served.

My nose scrunched. "I guess when you put it like that, it does sound kind of gross."

Lennon slid the saddle off, the bridle still looped over his arm, then passed me. I slid the door to the stall shut, then followed him to the tack room.

"You up for hanging around after everyone leaves?" he asked me as he set the saddle on a stand. He heaved a breath as he faced me.

"I don't want to impose…"

He pressed his lips together, studying me. "It's not imposing if I'm asking, Oakley."

My eyes dropped to his chaps and the snow lightly dusting his boots as I chewed on the inside of my cheek. I guessed he was right.

"That'd be nice. Thank you."

He nodded, then we headed back outside to watch the rest of the skiers do their laps.

***

The fire in the fireplace crackled as a log settled, sending sparks up the chimney. We all sat around the Bronsons' living room resting from the long day. Beckham had gotten home from his flight a few minutes before dinner. His friend had dropped him off here, and now he was enjoying a beer in the chair across from Reed.

People had skied for another hour after Lennon went, then we'd all mingled, talking about anything and everything. After Reed and Callan put the horses away, the neighbors had left and we all headed inside. We'd shed our snow clothes, leaving them to dry in the front entry. I was now in my white thermal and black leggings with my fuzzy socks pulled up past my ankles.

Charlotte had made pulled pork in the slow cooker, so we'd all sat around the table inside their home and ate, drank, and laughed. It felt good being around a family so large, being as I was an only child, and my only family was down in Colorado now.

After dinner, we'd all moved to the living room. Lennon was to my right on the couch, sitting next to Callan. Bailey and Lettie had taken the love seat, while Reed and Beckham sat in separate chairs by the bookcases. Brandy was sitting on the floor with her back to the coffee table, her feet outstretched as Lettie aimlessly swung her legs, tapping Brandy's socked feet. Charlotte sat perched on Travis's knee, his hand rubbing circles on her outer thigh.

"I still can't get over how far you flew when you fell, Cal," Bailey said through a laugh.

"He looked like a little snowball after," Lettie said, giggling from all the naughty hot chocolates.

"This is why you should always ride the horses," Reed murmured.

Callan sat back in his chair, not caring that they were practically picking on him for falling. "I almost liked the falling more than I did going around the track. Plus, Brandy here is slow," he teased.

Brandy sat forward, mouth agape. "Am not! You're just too much of a daredevil. Any faster and you would have broken a limb. I knew you were going to fall."

"Says the daredevil herself," Lettie shot at her.

Reed grunted from his chair with his arms crossed, but Brandy promptly ignored him. Beckham's gaze darted between everyone, a look of nostalgia crossing over his features. It was clear he missed his family when he was away, and even just watching them interact in person brought him joy.

My phone buzzed in my pocket on the side of my thigh, and I pulled it out, seeing a text from my dad.

> **Dad:** Divorce is being finalized today. Thought you should know.

My heart felt like it stopped in my chest. It was actually happening.

I knew the entire time that this was coming, but for some reason, I didn't expect it. I clicked the screen off and slid the phone back in my pocket.

"May I use the restroom?" I asked Lennon.

His brow furrowed as he studied my face. "Yeah. Down the hallway, third door on the right."

"Thanks," I said before getting up and making my way down the hall.

I didn't go into the bathroom. Instead, I leaned my back against the wall, looking up at the ceiling.

I was having such a good day, and it all came crashing down in an instant with one simple text. One small sentence. My family would never be the same again, and I hated that I had no choice but to accept it.

Inhaling a shaky breath, I swallowed the emotion lodged in my throat. I shook out my hands, forcing myself to get it together. It could still be a good day. I could act like I never got the text, but it'd be on the back of my mind regardless.

It'd been a long day anyway. I should make up some excuse and go home, but I hated cutting my time here because of my dad. I'd left Denver to get away from the effects of this whole thing between my parents, but it seemed it just followed me here.

22

LENNON

"So you thinking of retiring next year?" I asked Beckham from where I sat on the couch. The outside of my thigh was getting cold with the absence of Oakley next to me, and I wished she was back in the room already.

"Not sure," Beck replied. "I'm still young, and to be frank, I don't know what I'd do if I wasn't riding broncs."

"Could always be a rodeo clown," Bailey joked.

Beck shook his head. "I don't look good in makeup."

"You don't *have* to wear makeup," Lettie pointed out. "You just wear really bright colors and all that."

"Would you be a rodeo clown?" Beck questioned her.

"Well, no," she muttered, crossing her arms.

"My point exactly." He looked back to me as my parents sat to the left of him, eager to hear his answer. "I'll think about it, but I'm ninety-eight percent sure I'm doing another year at least."

Callan stayed quiet next to me, but I knew he wished he could convince him to quit. Hell, he'd probably even try to talk him into it before he left.

"Well, we support you either way," my mom piped in.

He gave her a soft smile. "Thanks, Mom." But he knew how much it worried them. One wrong move and he could break his neck or paralyze himself for life. He was riding a thin line where being safe was almost nonexistent.

My eyes moved to the empty spot next to me. I should go see if she's okay. Oakley looked like she was about to throw up when she asked if she could use the restroom. Last thing I wanted was for her to feel alone if she was sick or something.

"I'll be right back," I said to Callan before standing up and coming around the couch. I went to the fridge first to grab her a water bottle just in case she needed it, then headed toward the hall. As soon as I turned the corner, I found her leaning against the wall with her head cast down, staring at her lit up phone screen.

"Oak?"

Her head shot up and she clicked her phone screen off as her eyes met mine. She straightened, coming away from the wall a few inches.

"Sorry, I just needed a minute," she said quietly.

Making my way down the hall, I leaned against the wall opposite of her, holding the water bottle out to her.

"I brought this in case you needed it," I explained.

Was the hallway always this narrow?

"Thanks." She took the plastic bottle, but didn't uncap it.

"Sorry about them." I hiked my thumb toward the end of the hallway. "They can be a lot."

She shook her head. "No, they're great. It's not them. I love hanging out with them."

Love. She loved being around my *family?*

I ignored her choice of words as my brows pulled together. "What is it, then? Is everything okay?"

She sighed, then looked down, clicking on her phone screen and holding it out to me.

I read the text, then who it was from. Her dad.

Her parents were getting a divorce. Did she even know? Is that why she was here in Bell Buckle and not home in Denver?

I met her gaze as she lowered the phone. "Fuck, Oak. I'm so sorry. I had no idea."

She shoved the phone into the side pocket on her leggings. "It's okay. Nothing for you to apologize for."

My hand ran through my hair. I'd ditched my hat before we ate dinner.

"If you want some space, you can head home if you'd like," I offered.

Her eyes widened slightly. "Home?" she repeated.

"Is that where you want to be right now?" I asked.

Her teeth dug into her lower lip as she shook her head. "No, it's not."

My eyes caught on her mouth, watching the action. When I'd found her here a minute ago, she'd looked so damn sad, like she was battling some inner conflict with herself. But with just our small interaction, her mood seemed to already be shifting.

Now all the calls spamming her phone made sense. Her parents were probably trying to get ahold of her, and here she was, standing within arm's length of me.

I was so damn tired of beating around the bush when it came to what I really wanted with Oakley. She could drive back to Denver at any point, and I'd have missed the opportunity to know what it was like to be with her, to hold her, to feel those lips on mine, to fist my hand in her hair and have her neck exposed.

"Fuck it." I pushed off the wall, taking two long strides to close the distance between us, and crashed my mouth to hers as my hands came up to cup her cheeks. A small gasp escaped her lips, but she quickly met my pace as I slipped my tongue in her mouth. She tasted so damn good, but fuck, I already wanted more.

Her back hit the wall, and I slid my hands into her hair, angling her head back slightly for a better angle. Her hands slid up my chest to my neck, pulling me closer, like she couldn't get enough either.

I drew her bottom lip in between my teeth, eliciting a small moan out of her in response. Our hands were so lost on each other, I couldn't figure out where I wanted to touch her the most, but I knew I wanted it to be every inch of her body, and I wanted it to be now.

I couldn't hold back any more when it came to Oakley.

To my right, I heard a throat clear, but I ignored it. There was no fucking way anyone was ruining this right now.

"Lennon." Beckham's voice filled the hall from where he stood at the end of it.

Oakley pulled back instantly, assumingly not having heard him clear his throat before he spoke. She looked down at her socks, her cheeks a bright shade of red.

"Not now, Beck," I grumbled, dropping my hands to grab hers.

"Mom was looking for you. She mentioned something about baby pictures," he said before walking off with a knowing smirk on his face.

Oakley met my gaze, tilting her chin up. "We should go out there. I don't want to be rude."

I couldn't tell if she really wanted this to stop, but I didn't want to kiss her again if she truly did want to go back out there. But fuck, all I could think about was her lips back on mine, how she tasted, her gasp as her back hit the wall. I wanted more. All of her little gasps, her smooth lips on mine, her fingers grabbing at my neck.

People say perfect doesn't exist. But Oakley and me? That kiss we just shared? *That* was perfect.

"Alright," I said softly. "Do you want to talk about it?" Whether it was about her parents or that kiss or the fucking weather outside, I wanted her to know I'd listen.

She shook her head. "It's okay. I'd rather just enjoy the night."

I nodded, fighting the urge to kiss her again. "You just let me know when, and we'll talk."

She offered a small smile, but I wasn't entirely convinced. I wouldn't push her on it, though. I let go of one of her hands and led her down the hall, but before we got back to the living room, I dropped it, not sure if she wanted my entire family seeing us like that. For the rest of the night, I had to act like her mouth wasn't the only thing on my mind.

23

OAKLEY

"Good morning, Sage," I greeted as I walked into Bell Buckle Brews after stomping the snow off my boots outside. Having actual snow boots was way better than trying to make it with sneakers.

Sage smiled brightly back at me. "Good morning. Hurt yourself?"

I hadn't realized I was walking awkwardly until she mentioned it. I was sore from falling countless times while attempting to learn how to ski, and my gait showed it.

"Let's just say skiing is not my forte," I said once I got to the counter.

"You got to play in a fort? I wanna make a fort," Averly exclaimed as she hopped off her seat at one of the tables. I guess I hadn't seen her there.

"Not a fort, Avery. A forte," Sage corrected.

"What's a fort-ay?" Avery asked, doing her best to pronounce the word.

Sage pursed her lips, hiding a smile at her daughter's attempt. "Did you finish your sandwich?"

Avery nodded, then headed back to the table to grab her napkin. She proceeded to throw it in the trash by the front counter, then skipped to the bakery cabinet, eyeing the sweets.

Sage sighed, bringing her attention back to me. "What can I get you?"

"Black coffee, vanilla latte, and two cranberry scones, please." The least I could do after Lennon saved me from freezing to death on the side of the road, inviting me over to dinner at his parents' house, and giving me ski lessons was bring him a coffee and baked goods.

I had a lot of making up to do.

Sage typed it into the register, then turned to pour the black coffee after starting the espresso machine. While the espresso was brewing, she reached into the bakery cabinet to grab two scones. Avery tried to slip a hand in, but Sage was quick and closed the glass door, causing Avery to pout as she headed through the door to the back of the cafe.

"Sorry about her," Sage apologized as she placed the scones in a bag. "I'm still trying to find a babysitter. Surprisingly, there's not many in a town of maybe five hundred people," she joked, her voice laced with sarcasm. In towns this small, it was hard to come by much. I was grateful there was at least good coffee.

"It's no worries at all. She's adorable." I took the bag from her, then she set Lennon's coffee on the counter and got to work finishing mine.

"She sure is. All the elderly women who come in on Fridays for coffee go on and on about her." She faced the counter again, setting the steaming latte in front of me.

I handed her what I owed, then left a few dollars in the tip jar. "I'm sure they love her."

I didn't want to pry and ask where Avery's father was as it was none of my business, but a small part of me couldn't help but wonder.

She nodded. "Have a good day, Oakley. Tell Lennon I said hi."

I smiled. "You, too, Sage. I will. See you later."

I grabbed the two coffees and the bag of pastries, then headed for the door. The cold hit me in the face, instantly freezing my cheeks and the tip of my nose. I hurried to the feed store, thankful that the sidewalks were mostly empty as people stayed inside warm stores or at home during the cold mornings.

Snow that had blown in the wind overnight clung to the windows on shops, on top of lampposts, and piled high on the sides of the streets where snow plows had shoved it aside. The sun had just risen, casting a blue glow on everything through the slightly overcast sky.

I opened the door to the feed store with my shoulder, thankful that Lennon left it unlocked for me. We still had about ten minutes until the store opened, which gave me just enough time to warm up and scarf down my scone.

"Good morning," I greeted Lennon as I strolled through the doorway of his office.

His eyes raked over my body before meeting my gaze as I sat across from him. I placed the coffee and bag of scones on his desk, then took a long sip of my latte. Steam billowed up out of the tiny hole in the lid and swirled around my face as I sipped, warming my nose.

"Good morning." He phrased it more like a question. "You seem happy today, and... sore?"

I set my cup down, then stood to take off my denim coat that I'd thrown over my sweatshirt. It wasn't snowing today, so I'd opted not to wear a full-blown snow jacket, thinking this would keep me warm enough in the brief moments I'd be outside.

"Skiing is hard work," I pointed out.

He reached forward to grab his coffee. "Especially when you're spending more time falling than actually skiing," he pointed out with an eyebrow raise.

My hand found one of the scones in the bag and slid it out, bringing it to my lips to take a bite. Sage must put heaven in her pastries. I didn't think I'd ever tasted something this good before in my life.

"All a learning curve," I said after swallowing my bite and washing it down with a sip of my drink.

He took his scone out, flattening the bag to use as a makeshift plate. He set the pastry on it, then met my gaze. "Look, Oakley, about what happened in the hall-"

I waved my hand, dismissing him. "Don't worry about it."

"What?"

"I was vulnerable, you were concerned. It's okay." I didn't want him to feel bad about kissing me. He was probably having regrets. I mean, kissing your employee at your parents' house after teaching her how to ski and touching different parts of her body all day trying to help her balance? He practically had guilt written all over his face.

"Is that how you see it?" he asked.

I nodded, grabbing my latte and jacket as I stood from the chair. "It's all good. See you on the floor?" This was awkward, and I had to clock in anyway.

"Sure," he muttered, keeping his eyes on me as I left the room.

I really hoped things didn't get weird between me and Lennon at work. I had enough things to worry about in my life right now, and my boss firing me because he kissed me was not something I wanted to add to my list.

***

I was alone the majority of the day. Lennon had barely come out to take care of a few things, and then retreated back to his office to do God knows what.

In his defense, between him, Jacey, Leo, and myself, we kept the store in pristine condition, so there wasn't really a reason for him to be out here besides to take care of inventory, pricing, freight, or helping with the front if it was busy.

Speaking of freight, with it being busy yesterday, Jacey and Leo hadn't had the chance to finish unloading the bags of dog food, which was what I was working on in between customers. My body hated me for doing this after my other activities yesterday, but it had to be done. Other activities *not* including Lennon's mouth on mine and his hands in my hair.

Fuck. Maybe I shouldn't have interrupted him in his office this morning when he was trying to talk to me about the kiss. Maybe he didn't regret it, and he wanted to do it again.

Hell, *I* wanted to do it again.

He tasted like whiskey and cinnamon, though I'm sure today he'd taste more like black coffee and cranberries. I wasn't sure if I should tell him I didn't mean what I said, or stick to it. For all I knew, if I told him I didn't mean it, he'd tell me he actually did regret it, and I'd make an even bigger fool of myself.

I just didn't know how long I could hold myself back from kissing him again. Now that I knew what his lips felt like on mine, I wanted more.

I shouldn't have fucking played it cool in his office. I should have just shut up and let him speak, but of course, my lovely inability to stop talking when it was most important came out to play.

Bending at the knees, I hefted a fifty-pound bag of dog food up, hoping to make it onto the third shelf up from the bottom.

"Let me help you with that," a male voice said as the kibble started shifting the weight in the bag.

He grabbed the bag from me, tossing it on the shelf it belonged on. "Now why would they have a little lady like you doing all this hard work?" he asked, dusting his hands off.

I faced the bag, unwrinkling the material, then turned to the man.

Scooby Snack Guy.

"I'm usually okay with the bigger bags. I'm just sore today, is all," I said as a way of explaining that this *little* lady could handle bigger tasks. I wasn't going to say no to working just because some tasks were harder than others.

He raised an eyebrow, his gaze traveling down my body, then back to my face. "Sore, huh?"

I took a step back to give myself more space from him. "I tried skiing yesterday and let's just say, I won't be doing it again."

He chuckled, setting his hand on the metal shelf that he'd just set the bag on. "Skiing does take a lot of practice. I could teach you sometime."

I pasted on a small smile. "No, thanks. Like I said, I won't be doing it again."

"Bummer," he moped.

I inhaled a deep breath, sliding my hands into the back pockets of my jeans. "Was there something I could help you with? I kind of have to get back to…" I gestured to the bags on the dolly behind me.

"Just here for another bag of dog food," he said.

I reached to my right, grabbing the one I remembered I'd recommended to him. "You know, we have the bigger bag right here." I gestured to the one on the bottom shelf.

He shook his head, taking the small bag from my hands. "This one is perfect. My name's JP, by the way."

I didn't ask, but okay.

"Alright, JP, let me get you rung up and out of here before it gets dark out and the roads ice over."

Making my way around him in the aisle, I headed for the register, coming around the back of the counter. He set the bag in front of me, pulling out his wallet.

"Where were you skiing anyway? There's not any good slopes within an hour of here. You need speed to really get a feel for it," he said as he pulled out his card.

I scanned the bag, then clicked enter for the total to show up on his side. I didn't want to tell him where exactly I was because that was just creepy. "A friend's house."

He scoffed, inserting his card into the terminal. "That's why you kept falling. Your friend probably doesn't know how to ski. Guys try to act like they know everything."

"I never said it was a guy," I pointed out, staring at the buttons on the register.

He shrugged. "Figured it was. Probably wanted an excuse to touch you."

I met his gaze then. "Isn't that what you were doing?"

His brows furrowed. "What?"

"When you offered to teach me, is that not what you were doing? Trying to find an excuse to hang out with me and touch me?" God, I needed to shut up. The last thing I wanted to do right now was piss him off.

"No," he clipped, pulling his card out with a little too much force, then shoving it in his wallet. "Thanks for the dog food." He grabbed the bag and headed out of the store before the receipt finished printing.

I tossed the paper in the trash bin, then placed my hands on the counter with a sigh. I hung my head for a moment, then checked the clock on the wall. We closed in two minutes, and I was over interacting with customers for the day, so I walked around the counter to the door to lock it.

Maybe I did want an excuse for Lennon to put his hands on me again, but it wasn't going to be through skiing lessons.

24

LENNON

I pulled my hat off, running my hands through my hair, then fit the cap on backwards. I was tired of being in this stuffy office all day, but I didn't want to overstep my boundaries with Oakley again.

From our conversation this morning, it was clear she thought the kiss was a mistake, but all I could think about was her damn mouth and her little gasp. I wanted to make her gasp again, but for all different reasons.

Oakley appeared in the doorway, lightly knocking on the door jam twice to get my attention off my computer screen. "I'm ready to go," she stated as she entered the room with her hand on the knob.

"I'll be done in just a minute," I said as I looked back down at my computer screen to finish the report I was working on.

The door to my office clicked, and I looked up to find that she had closed it and was slowly prowling toward me like a cat stalking its prey. I watched as she came around my desk, the tips of her fingers trailing the top of it, before she twisted my chair so that I was facing her.

She used her leg to nudge my knees apart, stepping between them. Her hands trailed up my chest to my neck, wrapping around the back of it. My back hit the back of my chair as she lifted one leg, then the other, so she was straddling my lap.

"Oak," I warned. She didn't know what she was getting herself into like this. This position was too much. She was too vulnerable for me to take.

"You scared to kiss me now, cowboy? I thought you liked touching me," she practically purred.

My hands came up to grip her hips in case she got any ideas and started grinding on me.

"I did. I do, Oakley, but we shouldn't do this if you don't want it." I didn't want her to regret it again. Regret *me*.

"All I've been able to think about since you kissed me was your mouth, and I'm fucking aching, Lennon." Her lips were slightly parted as I tilted my head back to look up into her green eyes.

Something about that fucking look just did it for me. Fuck staying away.

"Tell me what you need, Oak. Anything, and I'll do it."

"Touch me," she whispered.

I shook my head. "You're in charge, baby. Tell me where."

She grabbed one of my hands from her hips, sliding it in between her legs.

I left my hand where she set it, but didn't move my fingers. My palm was pressed to her pussy, the fabric of her jeans separating us. "I want to hear you say it, Oak."

"I want you to touch my pussy," she said, her cheeks flushing as she clearly felt shy.

My palm pressed harder against her and that little gasp I fucking loved passed her lips. "Yeah? How do you want me to touch you here?"

She looked down at where my hand was pressed against her, biting her lip. "Without my jeans."

"Stand up," I instructed, reluctantly pulling my hand away from her.

She did, and I reached forward, working at the button and zipper to tug them off of her. I could see her wetness pooling in her panties, and my mouth filled with saliva at the urge to lick her clean. "Now come back," I said.

She obeyed, straddling me once again. She was wearing lavender-colored panties that were more lace than anything. I placed my palm back against her pussy just as it was before, awaiting her instruction.

She was so fucking hot against my hand, it was taking all I had in me to contain myself. "Tell me, Oak."

"In my panties," she whispered.

Slowly, I slid my hand down the front of her panties, finding her bundle of nerves immediately. I circled it, keeping my eyes on her as her eyelids flickered. Her hips bucked against my hand as I kept my attention on her clit.

"More," she said through a small whimper.

"How, baby?" I wanted to hear every word pass her lips. I wanted her in control because once she wasn't, I'd be in the lead, and I couldn't hold back once our roles reversed.

"Inside me." Her voice was so soft through her quick breaths.

"Beg for it."

Her eyes found mine as she continued moving her hips. "Please, Lennon. Please finger my sweet pussy. I want to feel your fingers inside me when I come."

I reached up to kiss her. "Good girl," I murmured against her lips at the same time I plunged two fingers inside her.

She gasped louder this time, her body jerking. "Fuck," she muttered.

I pumped her pussy with my fingers while my thumb put pressure on her clit, my entire hand soaked from her. "You're so fucking tight, Oakley. I don't think I can fit another."

"Please," she begged, her eyes on my hand as I worked her.

I adjusted my hand, squeezing in a third finger. She moaned, her head falling back as her hips kept lifting up and down with the pace of my hand. "That's my good fucking girl. Ride my hand, baby. Show me how you come."

"Lennon," she gasped as I quickened my pace, my thumb circling her clit quicker.

"What do you need, baby? Tell me." My cock was straining against my jeans right below where her pussy was and it took all I had not to rip my zipper open and fuck her with my cock instead of my hand.

Instead of using her words, she lifted the hem of her shirt until it was pulled up above her tits. She yanked the cup of her bra down, exposing one breast. I didn't need her words to know what she wanted.

I leaned forward the slightest bit, my mouth clamping down on her pebbled nipple. She moaned, holding nothing back.

She looked down at me as I stared up at her, relishing in how fucking perfect she was. She could ride my hand any fucking time and I'd let her as long as I got to see this part of her. Unhinged Oakley was now my favorite side of her.

"Bite it," she whispered, so softly I barely heard her. My teeth gently found the bud, adding a bit of pressure. Her head fell back as my fingers continued pumping her, eliciting another moan from her.

"Fuck, Lennon, I'm gonna come," she said, her voice breathy.

I kept my mouth on her nipple, a groan coming from my throat as I kept my pace with my fingers. Her limbs tensed, her pussy gripping my hand, making it almost impossible to keep my movements steady. Then all of a sudden, she released, her body falling forward as she muffled a scream in my shoulder, her teeth biting down on me as her body convulsed.

"Just like that, baby. Ride it out. Come for me," I said, my lips brushing her hair by her ear. My hand was so fucking soaked, I could feel the moisture on my jeans, but I didn't give a fuck. I wanted Oakley staining me everywhere.

Once I was certain she was done riding the waves of her orgasm, I gently removed my fingers from her pussy. Her mouth slowly unclamped from my shoulder as her breathing evened out.

Bringing my fingers up to my mouth, I wrapped my lips around them, getting a taste of her sweetness. Her heated eyes watched the movement as I sucked my fingers clean, then after removing them from my mouth, she crashed her lips to mine. Her tongue slid in like she wanted a taste, too, and fuck, if that wasn't the hottest thing.

She pulled back after we were both panting for breath, looking down at me.

"Tell me I can have you, Oakley," I murmured, my dry hand rubbing circles on her outer thigh.

She had a silent plea shining in her eyes, and whatever it was, I'd give it to her.

She nodded.

"Tell me I can fuck you right here," I begged.

She reached down to find my zipper, tugging it down along with undoing the button on my pants. She stroked her hand over my boxers, causing my cock to twitch. "The entire time, I imagined your fingers as your cock, and I'm not waiting another second to feel the real thing."

Her voice was laced with desire, and before she had the chance to tug my boxers down, I was lifting her off of me and kicking the chair out of the way. I flattened her chest to the desk so her ass was in the air. She was exposed for me, completely mine for the taking.

I didn't bother losing my pants or boxers. Instead, I slid the hem down just enough to free my cock, then lined it up with her entrance as I placed a rough palm on her lower back. I stroked the head to her clit, rubbing the sensitive bundle of nerves before sliding back to her entrance.

"Grab the desk," I ordered.

Her hands slid forward, her fingers curling over the edge of the desk in front of her.

My other hand ran circles on her ass, my fingers digging into her soft skin. "You're such a good girl, Oakley, taking my orders without even hesitating." I tapped a finger to her left leg. "Spread your legs wider, baby."

She shifted her leg, her body moving down just an inch with her spreading her feet wider apart.

My eyes studied her before me as I said, "I'm clean, but I can get a condom."

She shook her head. "I want to feel you. I'm on birth control."

I nodded, though I knew she couldn't see it. With a hand back on her lower back, I slowly slid in. My cock was soaked in seconds, her release still dripping out of her.

I pushed in a few more inches and she moaned, her head falling to the desk with a curse.

"I want all of it, Lennon. All of you."

I gripped her hips, burying myself in her. Once I was fully seated in her, I paused, giving her a moment to adjust to me.

"Please," she begged. "Please move, Lennon, or I'm going to explode."

I smirked. "Again?"

She shifted her hips back and I gripped them hard, keeping her in place. "Easy, baby. You're not the only one about to lose it."

She sighed like she was disappointed, so I did the only thing anyone would do. I slapped her ass.

The sound filled the room and she jumped slightly with a gasp. "Don't underestimate me, Oakley. I can go all damn night, but I can't say the same for you."

"Is that a challenge?" she murmured.

"If you want it to be, I'll make it happen." I started moving, slowly pulling out to the tip, then slamming back in. She moaned, her fingers white-knuckling the desk.

I wrapped one hand around her red hair, tugging her head back. Leaning over her back, I brought my lips to her ear, gently biting down on her earlobe as I continued thrusting in and out of her.

"You like it when your boss fucks you over his desk, Oakley?" I whispered in her ear.

Her head was still tilted back with her hands gripped tight to the desk. She shook her head as much as she could.

"No?" I questioned, keeping my pace. "You don't like how I feel inside this sweet pussy?" She'd be lying if she didn't. I could *feel* how much she loved it. How I made her body tighten and ache for more.

"No," she said through a breathy moan. "I like when *you* fuck me, Lennon."

"Same thing, baby."

She shook her head and I quickly pulled out to flip her around so her back and head were on the desk. Pushing myself back into her, I picked up speed again. Hovering over her, I grabbed her hands, pinning them above her head to the desk. Her mouth was parted, her hair fanned out around her, making her look all the more like a goddess.

She slowly clenched around me, and I knew what was coming. I kept my pace steady, thrusting into her deeper, so I hit that perfect spot inside of her that my fingers had found so easily. As soon as I hit it with my cock, she screamed, throwing her head back as her back arched. I let go of her hands, bringing my hands to the bend in her waist and holding her steady as I rode her through her orgasm.

"Just like that, baby. Come on my cock like you came on my fingers like the good girl you are."

"Lennon!" she screamed, her body twitching under mine.

My name on her lips was all it took to get there. I stopped, shoving deep inside her, then pulled out, emptying myself on her thigh and stomach. My hand supported me on the desk beside her hip as I hung my head, catching my breath.

"I was not expecting that," she said after a few moments.

I lifted my head to find her staring at me. "No?"

She shook her head. "Maybe older men have been the way to go all along."

I let out a small chuckle, shaking my head. "Don't go around saying that in town. They'll be flocking to you by the dozens."

She sat up, propping herself on her elbows. Her breasts were still on display with her shirt pulled up above them. "I don't want just any man, Lennon."

I stepped back, grabbing some tissues off my desk and cleaning her thigh and stomach up. After she was wiped clean, I tossed them in the trash bin on the floor and fixed my pants, then grabbed hers and bent to slide them over her feet. Once both legs were in, I pulled them up. She stood, making it easier for me to get them over her thighs and ass. After buttoning them, I fixed her bra and pulled the hem of her shirt down over her stomach.

Then, I grabbed her chin, tipping her head up to me. Those emerald eyes were heavy, her auburn hair mussed up, her freckled cheeks rosy. "Good. Because now that I've had you, I'm not letting any other man within five feet of you. You're mine. In every form of the word, you are mine. Got it?"

She nodded, and I bent slightly to press my lips to hers, kissing her gently. "That's my good girl," I whispered against her lips.

Goosebumps rose on her arms as I pulled back.

"So bossy," she muttered with a smile.

"When it comes to you, Oakley, I'll be bossy, but only when I need to make myself clear that you belong to me. I don't share."

Her cheeks deepened in color as she looped her arms around my neck. "You can boss me around all you want, cowboy."

I smirked. "You like that?"

She gave a little shrug, her smile deepening. "I might."

I brushed my lips across hers, still not having had enough of her. "I'll keep that in mind."

25

OAKLEY

Lennon pulled into the parking spot outside the shop, but as he reached for his key in the ignition, I grabbed his wrist, stopping him.

"You don't have to go in with me," I reminded him. We'd gone back and forth about it the entire ride here.

"Yes, I do," he said matter-of-factly.

I frowned. "And why's that?"

"What if for some reason your car isn't ready and then I have to come back to get you? Then I would have just wasted my time."

"He literally called you and told you it was ready," I pointed out. Apparently Wyatt, the shop owner, and Lennon were already friends, so he'd called him instead of trying to get ahold of me.

"Well, I want to look it over. Make sure everything is good to go," he said, twisting the key. The rumble of his engine faded away.

I blew a burst of air through my nose as he got out, coming around to my side. My arms were crossed when he opened the door, and at the sight of my stance, he raised an eyebrow.

"Sassy today, are we?" he teased.

It'd been three days since we had mind-blowing sex in his office, and aside from stolen kisses in the back hallway of the feed store, nothing had happened since.

He leaned in, setting a hand on the roof of the truck. "Do I need to cheer you up?"

I pursed my lips, trying to hold my attitude, but felt it slipping with the thought of Lennon on top of me in his truck. Or me riding his lap. Or doing literally anything with him, anywhere.

"No," I huffed, dropping my arms and swinging my legs to the door, coming to the edge of the seat.

My knees brushed his stomach and I looked up to find him smirking down at me. "Sure about that, Oak?"

My eyes drifted down to the bulge in his jeans. "Are *you* sure you want to walk in there with a boner?"

He shrugged like it was no big deal. "I know the guy."

I raised a brow, meeting his gaze. "Oh, does he want to join?"

He dropped the smirk, his eyes going hard as he leaned closer. "Remember what I said, Oak? I don't share."

"Then maybe you shouldn't be trying to have sex with me in a parking lot," I pointed out, the last half of my sentence coming out in a whisper.

"Oh, I don't care if people watch. But they can't fucking touch what's mine," he said, his voice low and full of possession.

I looked around us. "I don't know, I don't really *feel* like I'm yours. It's been three days-"

His hands gripped my hips, yanking me forward as a yelp escaped my lips. I had to set my hands on his chest to keep from colliding with him. "You need me to remind you?"

I gulped, my belly doing somersaults at the thought of him inside me again. I nodded slowly, too afraid to speak because I wasn't sure if I could form words with the way he was looking at me like he wanted to devour me.

"Let's get your car, and then I'll remind you how it feels when I'm inside you."

I nodded again, and he took a step back, grabbing my hand to help me out of his truck.

He closed the passenger door for me and we headed inside, the bell above the door dinging as we entered the small lobby area. There were four gray chairs that matched the gray carpet, and a desk at the end of the narrow room that held two computer monitors and a large calendar flat on the desk.

Behind the desk sat a man with dark wavy hair that curled at the nape of his neck. He wore a dark gray button up with the shop's logo on the tiny pocket. "Hey, guys."

"How's it goin', Wyatt? This is Oakley," Lennon introduced me.

Wyatt looked up from his computer, giving me a big smile. "Nice to meet you, Oakley."

"You, too." I smiled back.

"So," he started, laying a piece of paper on the desk facing me and Lennon. "Fuel pump was bad, so I replaced that. And I took care of your other request, Len. Car's all good to go."

My brow furrowed as I approached his desk, looking down at the paper. "Other request?" I muttered in question.

I skimmed the information, finding exactly what he meant. "New tires?" I twisted to face Lennon. "Lennon, I can't afford that right now."

"They're already paid for," Wyatt said.

I spun to look at him. "Paid for? By who?"

"Me," Lennon said from behind me.

I twisted again, convinced I was going to get whiplash. "I don't need you to pay-"

A phone ringing behind me cut me off. Wyatt answered it with a quick, "Yello."

I didn't finish what I was saying, not wanting to be rude to him as he was on the phone, but I kept my eyes on Lennon, staring him down and hoping he knew what I really wanted to say.

That I couldn't let him buy me an entire brand new set of tires.

I mean, sure, my old tires had pretty much no tread left on them, and these new tires would help immensely in the snow, but that wasn't a cheap purchase.

"I'll be right out," Wyatt said into the phone before I heard him set it down, having ended the call. "I've got a tow truck about five minutes out with a car I need to help him unload into the back. You guys want the keys to the Subaru so you can head out?"

Lennon shook his head, keeping his eyes on me. "No, we'll wait for you, Wyatt."

What? Why?

"Alright, be back in a jiffy," Wyatt said before I heard a door click behind me from where I was still facing Lennon.

"Why don't we just go?" I asked.

Lennon slowly stalked toward me until I had to step back, my ass connecting with the desk behind me. He set both hands on the desk, caging me in. "I think it's time to remind you of a couple things."

"What?" I squeaked.

In one swift motion, he twisted his hat backwards and grabbed my hips, lifting me so I was now sitting on the desk.

"But Wyatt's outside. What if he comes back in?" I stuttered.

"It won't take me that long to make you come," Lennon stated.

My jaw dropped.

"Careful." He set a finger under my chin, closing my mouth for me. "Don't give me any ideas. We only have a few minutes."

"Then what're you taking your time for?"

His hands instantly went for the button on my jeans, undoing it along with my zipper. In one swift motion, he had them off and laying in a heap on the ground. He grabbed my ankles, wrapping my legs around his torso, then slid his hands up my legs, lifting me completely off the desk. "Hold on, sweetheart."

My legs tightened around him as he took the few steps to the wall, propping my back against it. There was no point in telling him no, not that I wanted to anyway, so I reached between us, working at the button and zipper on his jeans.

With my body between him and the wall, Wyatt wouldn't be able to see any exposed parts of me even if he did walk in, but I had a feeling Lennon was going to keep his promise and I'd be screaming his name within the next two minutes.

Lennon kept one hand on my ass and slid the other between us, shoving aside my panties and lining the tip of his cock up with my entrance.

Before I had the chance to brace myself, he was sliding in fast, burying himself as deep as he could go. I gasped, my fingers digging into the skin on the back of his neck. He lowered his head to kiss my neck, gently biting my skin. My head fell back against the wall as he thrusted in and out of me with his hands gripped tight on my ass.

A moan escaped my lips despite my attempt to stay quiet, knowing there were people outside. Lennon felt so damn good, and I wanted nothing more than to feel him inside of me every fucking day.

"You like my cock in your sweet little pussy, Oak?" he panted.

I hummed a response, unable to form words.

"Say you're mine," he demanded.

"I'm yours," I said, my voice breathy.

One of his hands released my ass, and in a breath, his hand was fisted in my hair, pulling my head back further so my neck was exposed.

"So fucking perfect. All wet and ready for me, like you've wanted me to fill your pussy ever since I last made you come."

My lips parted as he continued fucking me.

"Rub that pretty clit, Oakley," he instructed.

Sliding one hand down his chest and keeping the other looped around the back of his neck, my fingers found that bundle of nerves and began rubbing circles as I already felt the pressure building low in my belly.

"That's my good girl. I want to feel you come on my cock. Want to feel your pussy choke me when you let go."

He thrusted deeper, hitting that blissful spot inside of me. After a few more thrusts, I exploded, my entire body tensing around him as the wall and his body were my only support.

"Just like that, baby."

Stars exploded behind my eyes, and I thought I might explode right along with them as he kept his pace. A loud moan escaped my lips and I quickly pursed them shut, trying to keep my orgasm quiet, which was proving to be almost impossible with Lennon.

After I was able to relax my body, he pulled out, keeping me wrapped around his waist.

"Aren't you going to come?" I asked, nervous that it didn't feel good to him.

He smiled. "Baby, that'd be a mess that I don't think we have time to clean up right now."

"What?" I asked, scared that he somehow knew Wyatt was about to walk in.

"Drive safe!" I heard a muffled voice from outside yell out as tires crunched over slushy snow in the parking lot.

I cursed and he dropped me, grabbing my jeans and handing them to me. As I quickly fixed my panties and slipped my jeans on, he situated himself back into his pants.

Right as I was finishing with the button on my jeans, the handle on the door twisted and Wyatt came walking in.

"Sorry 'bout that, guys. Thankfully, it didn't take too long, though," Wyatt said, closing the door and then turning to face us.

He knew.

The look on his face and the way the corners of his mouth twitched, I knew that he knew.

My hair probably looked like a bird had been trying to make a nest in it after Lennon had his fist in it.

I huffed out a breath, trying to calm my nerves. "So, the Subaru?" I asked, trying to sound casual, but sounding the complete opposite.

"Right," Wyatt said, grabbing the keys behind his desk. "The car."

26

LENNON

After picking up Oakley's car, I'd followed her back to Tumbleweed Feed. We were the only two scheduled today, but since our trip to the shop took longer than expected, I'd called Leo and Jacey to open the store for me.

Though Leo had grumbled about it on the phone, he'd shown up. I let them both leave after we'd arrived so they could have the rest of the day off.

I didn't know what I'd do without Jacey and Leo.

Now I could add Oakley to that list, too.

She'd been so damn flustered after Wyatt came back inside, her cheeks the deepest shade of crimson I'd seen them yet.

It was like she had "I just had sex in your waiting room" written across her forehead for him to see.

Wyatt was no fool to flustered women with his good looks and all, but even he knew it wasn't about him.

Oakley's hair was sticking up in odd places, though she'd tried to run a finger through it multiple times. Another tell-tale sign that she'd just had sex.

I'd have to work on her post-sex poker face with her if I wanted to take her more places.

Being in public wouldn't stop me from putting my hands on her, and I'd proven as much this morning at the shop.

Something about Oakley made me give in to my primal need to stake my claim on her and show everyone who she belonged to.

I was working on redoing an endcap when I glanced over at Oakley behind the register, talking with Margaret. That old woman would talk her ear off if I didn't rescue her.

Setting the paper on the shelf, I ambled over to them, placing my hands on the edge of the counter. "Good morning, Marg," I greeted with a smile.

"You're looking handsome today, young man," she acknowledged, looking me up and down.

"Opposed to any other day?" I joked.

My hat was still backwards for the sole reason that Oakley liked it that way. I wasn't a fool. I knew why she got so flustered every time it was turned around.

Margaret waved me off, grabbing her purse and bag of bird seed off the counter. "Cocky, too."

I feigned hurt, pressing a hand to my chest. "Ouch."

"She's right," Oakley admitted with a small smile.

My gaze moved to her and her cheeks flushed, causing a smirk to bloom on my mouth.

"You two take care," Margaret called over her shoulder as she headed for the door.

I hadn't even noticed the lady had started walking away.

"Cat got your tongue?" I raised an eyebrow at Oakley.

She narrowed her eyes before moving to go around the counter. I caught her elbow, pulling her to my chest and caging her in with both hands on the counter on either side of her.

Her pink lips parted as she angled her chin up at me.

"You've barely said a word to me since we've been here. What's wrong?" I asked. Something had to be up. It was a few hours from closing at this point, and she couldn't keep avoiding me all day.

"Nothing's wrong."

I pinned her with a look.

She sighed, resting her ass against the lip of the counter. "Okay, fine. Do you think Wyatt knew?"

I tried to hide my laugh, pursing my lips together.

"What?" she exclaimed.

"He knows, Oak."

She dropped her hands in exasperation. "Just great."

"What? You don't want him to know you're sleeping with me?" She had no image to uphold with Wyatt. Hell, she barely knew the guy.

"No. It's just awkward," she stated.

"You see him often?" I questioned. I knew she didn't.

She narrowed her eyes again. "No."

"Then you have nothing to worry about."

"Maybe we should keep this," she waved a hand between our chests, "in the bedroom."

I leaned in close, my face mere inches from hers. "I haven't even had you in the bedroom yet. But regardless, this," I waved my hands between us, mimicking her movements, "is not a secret. *We* are not a secret."

"We work together," she pointed out.

I grabbed her chin with my thumb and forefinger, tilting her chin up further to be sure she saw me when I said, "And I'm the boss. I'll fuck my employee whenever and wherever I please."

Her cheeks flushed, but whatever she was about to say was cut off by my phone ringing in my back pocket.

Dropping her chin and taking a step back, I pulled my phone out, seeing it was Callan.

"What's up?" I said into the phone after answering.

"Got a few hours to spare?" Cal asked.

"Why?"

Oakley watched me as I stood a few feet in front of her.

"Got some cows out on the road, and it just so happens that everyone besides me and Dad are busy." He sounded irritated, like they'd been working on the issue for a while and finally decided to bring in backup.

I checked my watch, seeing that it was two and a half hours from closing.

"I can be there in a half hour. I just have to call someone in to cover until closing."

Oakley held up a finger. "I can close."

I shook my head, angling the phone away from my mouth while keeping it pressed to my ear. "No fucking way."

"You don't trust me?" she asked, a bit of disappointment ringing in her tone.

"I do, baby. But you're not closing alone. I'll call Leo," I said to her.

"Baby?" Callan repeated in my ear.

"I'll text you when I'm leaving," I muttered to Callan before hanging up the phone and dialing Leo.

He answered on the third ring. "Let me guess, you need me to come back in."

"I wouldn't ask if I didn't need you."

Oakley went back behind the register, fiddling with little items like pens and sticky notes as she waited for me to get off the phone.

"I can be there in ten minutes," Leo said.

"Thanks, Leo. I owe you." I ended the call, sliding my phone back in my pocket.

"Everything okay?" Oakley asked, looking up at me.

I nodded. "Just some cows out on the road. Hopefully won't take too long to get it sorted out."

"Be safe," she said softly.

"Worried about me, Oak?" I teased.

She rolled her eyes. "Since you're my boss and my... whatever you are, yes, I am."

"Your boyfriend," I filled in. Though less than two minutes ago, I'd called her my employee, I realized now that I wanted her to be more than just that. I wanted a title. I wanted dates, to bring her flowers, to take her out dancing, to bring her chocolates during her time of the month.

"That's not how that works," she stated.

"Oh, you want to get all traditional now?" We'd already had sex, twice, and I wasn't about to let her get away from me now.

She shrugged. "I guess I do."

If that's what she wanted, I'd give it to her. "Alright."

"Really?" she asked, disbelief seeping into her tone.

I nodded once. "If that's what you want, I'll do it."

The bell on the door dinged as Leo passed through the entrance, bundled in a big navy blue snow jacket. He pulled his gloves off, shoving them into his pockets. "I'll just set my stuff in the break room and I'll be right up here."

"Thanks, Leo," I said to him.

"Yeah, yeah." He walked by me, heading for the back of the store.

"I'll call you when I'm done at the ranch," I told Oakley.

I bent down, cupping her cheek and pressing a kiss to her lips. God, just kissing her did crazy things to me.

"Tell Cal and your dad I said hi."

"Will do." I headed for my office to grab my jacket and keys, wishing I didn't have to leave Oakley at the store.

At least it would give me time to think of how I wanted to make this official with her.

27

LENNON

When I'd pulled up to the ranch, Callan already had my horse ready for me to hop on and head out. Our dad was still out with the cows on the road, doing his best to keep them out of traffic. They were stubborn in this cold, and with the snow drifts piled high, they were acting like they couldn't get back through the fence.

"It's about damn time," Dad grumbled as we approached from the field.

"I have this thing called a job," I reminded him.

He grunted, twisting his horse around to keep a straggler in check.

Callan led his buckskin, Ace, through the snow drift, which had been trampled in one narrow spot from the cows when they got out of the pasture.

"Think we need to shovel it?" Callan asked as he observed the narrow passageway.

Our dad scoffed. "You wanna wash their assholes and paint their hooves while you're at it?"

I let out a bark of laughter. Our dad always took great care of the cattle, but he wasn't about to treat them like a house pet.

"It's a little bit of snow. They walked through it to get out here in the first place," Dad said, looking both ways on the dark road for headlights.

I eyed the snow drift. "It's probably four feet tall. That isn't small, Dad."

"At least it ain't ten," he grumbled.

Always looking on the bright side.

I led my horse, Winston, through the snow drift, the cows parting to move away from him. Once on the other side, I pivoted, getting behind the ass of one of them and whistling through my teeth, the sound piercing the air.

The cows got moving, but instead of going back through the narrow passageway in the drift, they just shifted around like they were blocked in.

Callan joined me as our dad stayed watching for traffic, waving his hands to keep the runaways with the group. As we hooted and hollered, ushering them closer and closer to the passageway, one finally got the brains to stick her head through the opening.

"C'mon, Mama. That's it," I urged her.

As if she understood my words, she made the jump, landing on the other side. The others began following suit, the passageway getting wider as packs of snow fell on their backs.

"Always gotta be a show-off, don't you?" Callan said.

I shrugged. "Don't be jealous."

Thankfully, the whole herd of them didn't escape and it was just a small bunch, otherwise we'd need every helping hand we could get. Once the last one ambled its way through, the three of us followed suit. Cal and our dad dismounted, getting to work on the fence that had somehow collapsed in one spot.

I stayed on Winston in case any of the cows got the bright idea to try to escape again, but I had a good feeling they wouldn't be wanting to cross that snow drift anytime soon.

"*Baby*, give me a hand," Callan mocked.

I narrowed my eyes at his back where he was bent over. "Got something to say, Cal?"

Dad moved his gaze to Cal. "Did you just call your brother *baby*?"

"I need the wire cutters from my bag," Cal said over his shoulder, ignoring our dad.

I swung my leg over, dismounting from Winston. Keeping the reins in my hand, I trudged through the snow to the saddle bag attached to Ace's saddle, fishing around for the wire cutters.

With a gloved hand, I grabbed them, bringing them over to Callan with Winston ambling along behind me. "Here you go, *baby*."

"What the fuck is going on?" Dad demanded.

Cal chuckled under his breath as he moved his focus back to the barbed wire. "Len's got a lady."

"Is that lady you? Because why the hell else would you be callin' your brother pet names?"

A snort escaped me.

With the moon lighting up the snow covered ground, I could see Cal shake his head. "No, Dad."

Our dad stood, bending his back to stretch it from being bent over. "Is it that employee you brought to the house?"

"Sure is." I couldn't keep the smile off my face.

"I knew you were full of shit," he muttered, coming around to the side of his horse and grabbing the horn of the saddle to pull himself up. He swung a leg over, situating himself in the saddle.

I shrugged. "Couldn't keep my hands to myself."

"I'd say you never could, but that'd be a lie. She must be special." He leaned an arm on the horn while Callan finished up the last bit of the fence.

I threw the split rein back over Winston's neck, then hefted myself back up on him. "She sure is."

"That doesn't explain this whole *baby* thing, though," he pointed out.

Cal stood, grabbing the few supplies with him as he stomped through the snow to Ace. "Lennon went all alpha mode on the phone when I called him to come help."

"Alpha mode?" Dad and I questioned in unison.

Cal nodded as he organized the supplies on his horse, stuffing tools in the saddle bag. "*You're not closing alone*," he said in a mocking tone.

"I care about my employees." It was true. And I wasn't about to leave her alone there because I had something I needed to do.

"You mean you care about Oakley," Cal corrected. He mounted Ace, then spun him around to start heading through the field.

He was right.

But I cared about Leo and Jacey, too. It was just a different kind of care that I had for Oakley now. Like if anything happened to her, I'd stop at nothing to make sure she was okay.

My dad was on the opposite side of Cal as we made the trek back to the barn. Thankfully, it wasn't snowing, but the foot or so of snow still stuck to the ground made it a slow hike back.

It took everything in me not to urge Winston into a gallop to get across this field and to my truck where my phone was so I could call her. Hear her voice. Feel the way she made my heart stutter.

28

OAKLEY

"All done," Leo said as he threw the planogram sheet into the drawer under the register.

He'd been working on the planogram Lennon had left for him to do and had just finished it with ten minutes to spare before closing.

"Thank God you did it because those sheets look confusing." It was all pictures and random numbers, none of it making sense to me with the glances I took at the sheets while Jacey, Leo, and Lennon did them here and there.

He gathered the spare supplies he'd set on the counter, now standing on the opposite side of the register facing me. Thankfully, the end of the day had been slow, with only a few customers coming in after Lennon left.

"When you've done over a hundred of them, it's pretty easy. Just tedious. Do you mind if I head out a few minutes early? I have a package I need to get in the mail for my sister."

"Yeah, of course. Something special?" I asked. I didn't mind him leaving early, and it really wasn't my place to tell him no.

He smiled, clear that thoughts of his sister made him happy. "Yeah. She's been looking for this record, and I found it yesterday at this little shop. I was going to send it out earlier today, but you know…" Then he was called in to cover.

"You better get it there quick, then. I'm sure she's antsy to listen to it."

"It's a surprise. I can't wait to hear her scream into the phone when it shows up on her doorstep."

I grinned. "I bet. Package it with, like, forty feet of bubble wrap."

"Oh, don't worry, I will. It'd kill me if it broke in shipping. Thanks, Oakley. Get home safe, alright?"

"I will."

He headed for the back of the store with the spare supplies, and about two minutes later, he was walking out the front door with his coat and beanie on. "Night, Oakley."

"Goodnight, Leo," I replied.

While I waited for the clock to tick down the minutes until I could lock the doors, I faced some shelves of rabbit and chicken feed. I wasn't expecting anyone to come in a few minutes before closing, but I stayed by the front just in case.

Hopefully Lennon wasn't out too long in the cold trying to round up the cattle. I was antsy to be off and to possibly see him tonight.

I'd never had sex in a public place before, and with Lennon, it was seeming to become a habit. It was like we couldn't resist the temptation of each other, and being out wasn't going to stop us from giving in.

We'd been beating around the bush of our obvious attraction to each other for what felt like forever, and now that we'd finally crossed that line, there was no going back. Not that I'd even want to go back anyway.

I hadn't been expecting to find solace in this small town when I'd arrived here, but slowly, it was starting to feel like a home. I had the job, the makeshift house, the guy. There wasn't much more I was seeking out of life besides being happy, and after a long time of feeling like I'd never feel that way again when my parents separated, I was finally starting to feel joy again.

It was hard to put into words how it felt when the world you'd always known came crashing down in front of you. I'd never thought I'd be a twenty-four-year-old being brought into the middle of my parents' divorce, and as much as I wanted to stop it, to keep my parents together in the hopes we could all fall into that comfortable world again, it wouldn't make the past year disappear.

And now that I was finding a home in Bell Buckle, making friends and enjoying my job, part of me didn't want the bad to go away. My mom cheating was a shock, their divorce inevitable, but without all of that, I would have never ended up here. I would have never met Lennon or his family; probably never would have even stepped foot in Bell Buckle.

As much as we hated the bad times in our lives, sometimes they had outcomes you'd never expect, and if you were lucky, they'd lead to some of the best moments of your life.

Meeting Lettie at that booth all those weeks ago and Lennon hiring me? That was luck. But Lennon and I becoming more than coworkers? That was fate. Like all my life, every small thing that happened was leading up to these bigger, life-changing events.

Heading out of the aisle to the front door, I twisted the lock, then went around the back of the register to grab the till. I made my way to the office, balancing the till in one hand. Leaving the door open, I sat behind Lennon's desk and got to work counting the money and doing the closing duties he left on a list by his computer. I already knew what to do since he'd shown me multiple times, probably just for an excuse to be close to me, but I referenced the list anyway to make sure I didn't skip anything.

As I was placing the bag of money in the safe under his desk, I heard a bang from out in the store, like something had hit the edge of a shelf.

I froze, peeking up over the desk from where I was still bent toward the safe. "Hello?" I called out.

Maybe it was Lennon getting back from the ranch and he came here instead of calling me since we had just closed.

But instead of Lennon's voice, I was met with silence. I slowly stood from the chair and approached the door of the office, peeking my head out into the hall.

There hadn't been anyone in the store when I locked the doors, so it couldn't be a customer. The bell over the door hadn't chimed for the last hour, at least.

Slowly inching my way down the hall, careful to keep my steps light, I peered around the corner, checking both sides but seeing nothing. The lights in the store dimmed after closing, so it wasn't exactly bright in the store, but I still couldn't make out anyone from where I was standing.

"Is there someone in here?" I called out, my voice echoing throughout the store.

Another clang sounded from a few aisles over and I yelped, spinning on my heel and running back to the office. I didn't care if the sound came from a goddamn mouse, my heart was pounding out of my chest with the fear that it was more than that.

I slammed the office door shut, my fingers fumbling over the lock. Over the sound of my heart beating in my ears, footsteps sounded somewhere in the store, and then a crash, like glass being broken.

Swallowing the scream that threatened to escape, I launched for the work phone on the desk, my fingers shaking as I tapped out 9-1-1.

"9-1-1, what's your emergency?" The feminine voice over the line wasn't soothing, despite her calm tone. Something about having to call an emergency number made my heart pound faster, my knees threatening to fold.

"I-I think someone broke into Tumbleweed Feed," I stuttered into the phone.

"Are you in the store right now?" she asked.

I nodded, then remembered she couldn't see me. "I am. I'm locked in the back office."

"We'll send someone right now. Stay in the office and do not open the door. Are you safe in there?"

"Yes."

"The officer is two minutes out. I'm going to stay on the line with you, okay?"

"Okay," I said through a whimper I tried to hide.

"What's your name?" she asked.

"Oakley Rae."

"Alright, Oakley. Hang in there. He'll be there soon."

I hoped the glass breaking was them leaving the store, but I wasn't going to risk it by going out there.

My cell phone was in the break room, so I couldn't call Lennon while I was on the line with dispatch. God, if they shattered the front window, he'd have to pay to get it fixed. I should have just left the front door unlocked so they had an easier escape and didn't resort to breaking a window.

"The officer just arrived. Backup is on the way. He's going to clear the store, then come to you, okay? Just stay put."

"Okay." There was silence, and then what felt like an eternity later, a voice spoke up through the door.

"Oakley?" a male voice called through the door.

"Yes," I replied, my voice shaky.

"This is Officer Archer. You can open the door now. There's no one here."

"You can hang up with me now," the woman on the phone said.

"Thank you for your help." I set the phone down, ending the call, then moved to the door, slowly unlocking it and twisting the handle.

A tall, dark-haired man stood on the other side in full uniform. "Are you feeling okay? Hurt anywhere?" he asked.

I shook my head, opening the door further. "No. I'm okay. Was it a break-in?"

He nodded, his eyes searching mine, which I knew were wide with fear. "Looks like it. If you want to head outside with me, I can get you checked out while you answer a few questions?"

I nodded, my hands still shaking as I held onto the doorknob.

He led me out of the office toward the front of the store, and as we approached the ambulance that was now sitting outside, I realized I'd forgotten my phone in the break room.

"Can you call Lennon? Tell him what happened?" I asked Officer Archer.

"Another officer already did. Left him a voicemail," he replied.

He was still out on the ranch, oblivious to what was happening here.

Instead of feeling relieved that the police were here, all I wanted was to be in Lennon's arms, to have his safety net thrown around me like a blanket.

29

LENNON

Latching the gate on Winston's stall, I headed out of the barn, eager to get to my phone to call Oakley and let her know I was done here.

"You wanna stay for a beer?" Cal asked, coming up beside me as I approached my truck.

"Not tonight. Maybe tomorrow?"

"Tomorrow's good with me. Hey, thanks for coming out here tonight. I know it's hard with the store and all to make time to come out, but we really appreciated the extra hand with those cows."

"'Course, Cal. I'll always come if you need the help." I opened the driver's door, reaching in for my phone on the seat.

Lighting up the screen, I saw a missed call and one voicemail from an unknown number. Cal stayed by me as I held the phone up to my ear, playing the voicemail.

"Hey, Lennon. This is Officer Brandon. There was a break-in at Tumbleweed Feed. The girl's okay, Officer Archer is inside with her now. Gonna get her checked out, but when you get the chance, give me a call back."

Then it ended.

And my blood froze in my veins.

"What is it?" Callan asked, seeing the fear on my face.

Was she hurt?

Where was Leo?

"The store. Someone broke in." It was all I could manage to get out. I hopped in the truck and Callan came around the passenger side, jumping in with a muttered curse.

"Was Oakley there?"

I turned the key with so much force I thought it might snap in half, then threw it into drive, gripping the steering wheel like it could make the old truck go faster. I gunned it down the drive, barely slowing as I turned onto the main road.

"Yes. But Leo was supposed to fucking be there, too." If something happened to her because Leo fucking left...

"They said he wasn't?" He'd come to the conclusion who had left the voicemail.

"Didn't fucking mention anyone other than Oakley, so no. Doesn't sound like he was." My voice was deadly, but Cal didn't shrink back. He knew I cared deeply about the people in my life, and someone having been in danger when I couldn't do anything to stop it tore at me the same way it would him. Callan and I loved deeply and cared fiercely, with all our being. We were the closest out of our other siblings for that very reason.

My tires screeched on the pavement as I made the turn to head into town, speeding down the road faster than anyone should be going. I didn't give a fuck if I got a speeding ticket. I'd take a thousand of those if it meant making sure Oakley was okay.

A few minutes later, I slammed on the brakes, stopping a few feet in front of a police cruiser. There was a firetruck, an ambulance, and two police SUVs sitting out front of the store, filling the parking lot.

I jumped out of the truck, my gaze immediately finding Oakley sitting on the back of the ambulance. My heart dropped seeing her sitting there, curled under a blanket, looking so damn small and vulnerable.

I ran to her, her eyes shooting up when she realized it was me.

"Oakley," I said her name like a plea, wrapping my arms around her and holding her to my chest. She shook in my arms, her limbs trembling. "Are you hurt?"

She shook her head against my chest, her red hair falling out from under the blanket.

Callan was talking to an officer a few feet away from us while I held her.

Her voice was muffled by my shirt as she said, "I'm sorry, Lennon, the window-"

"I don't give a damn about the fucking window, Oakley. I just want to know you're okay." I wouldn't be able to breathe until I knew for sure she was unharmed.

"I'm okay," she said into my chest.

My hand stroked down the back of her head, my fingers brushing through her hair. "Where's Leo?"

She looked up at me, those green eyes glazed over. "It's not his fault."

My jaw clenched. "It is."

She reached up to cup my cheeks, the blanket still draped over her shoulders being held up by my arms around her. I wouldn't let her go. Didn't think I could if I tried.

"It would have happened if he was here or not."

I searched her eyes, trying to convince myself she was okay. "You could have been hurt."

"But I wasn't. I'm okay," she said softly, her thumb stroking my cheek.

But she wasn't okay. She was fucking scared, and I could see it in her eyes, feel it in the way her hands shook against my skin.

I wrapped my arms around her tighter, guiding her head back to my chest. She dropped her hands from my face, wrapping them around my waist.

Callan came up beside us, looking over Oakley for a brief second before moving his attention to me. "The guy left before the cops got here."

My jaw tightened, my teeth threatening to break. "Did they check the cameras?"

He nodded. "He was wearing a black hoodie with the hood drawn, so they couldn't see much. He came in through the door in the back next to the roll-up door for freight."

I cursed, looking down at Oakley's red hair against my chest as she looked at Callan. "That's why I didn't hear the bell go off."

A muscle in Callan's jaw twitched. "He picked the lock on the door, and without the alarm set yet, you would have never known. He must've broken the window for an easier escape."

Tears pooled in her eyes, the lights on the vehicles reflecting in them.

I wanted her out of here.

"Is she cleared to go?" I asked the paramedic by the back of the ambulance.

He nodded. "All good."

I turned to Cal. "Can you drive her car home?"

Oakley looked up at me. "I can drive."

I shook my head, meeting her gaze. "I'm taking you to my place."

"Yeah, I'll have Dad pick me up," Cal said.

"Thank you," I told him.

"I don't want to inconvenience him," Oakley said to me.

I brushed her hair out of her face, then bent to kiss her forehead, closing my eyes as I murmured, "You're not inconveniencing anyone. Let me take care of you."

She fisted her hands in my shirt, the trembling nearly gone now. "Okay," she whispered. "My things are in the break room."

"I'll get them," Cal offered.

"Thanks," I said.

Cal turned to head inside to get her belongings from the break room, reappearing a few minutes later with her phone, coat, and keys. "Thank you," she said quietly, taking the coat and phone from him.

I still had her pressed against me, too scared to let her go, like she might crumble if I did.

"You two get home safe."

"Let me know when Dad picks you up," I said to him.

"Will do." He headed for her Subaru in the corner of the lot.

I tipped my chin, looking down at her where she was watching Cal cross the lot. "I'm taking you to my house tonight."

Her eyes moved to mine. "Lennon, I said I don't want to inconvenience-"

I cupped her cheek, shaking my head. "You're anything but an inconvenience, Oak. I want nothing more than for you to stay at my place tonight, break-in or not." She was shaken up by the whole thing, and I wasn't about to let her be alone at her place tonight.

Retail stores were broken into all the time. Not as frequently in small towns like Bell Buckle, but regardless, as much as I didn't want to assume it was a targeted attack, you could never be too safe. I'd make sure the police found whoever did this, and if they didn't make them pay, I would. No one got to scare my girl and get away with it.

"Okay," she whispered, her eyes dropping like any fight had left her.

"Do you have everything you need from here?" I'd figure out the window when we got home. The police had already taped it off, so it wasn't an immediate concern of mine. Right now, all I cared about was Oakley. My focus was solely on this redheaded, freckle-cheeked woman in my arms, and I couldn't be bothered with anything else.

She nodded, then dropped her head to my chest again, leaning against me. The adrenaline of the break-in must have exhausted her.

"Let's go home, baby," I murmured, pulling her to my side so we could walk to my truck.

I helped her into the passenger seat, then came around to the driver's side, starting up the truck and heading out of the parking lot. The entire ride home, she was slumped in her seat, fiddling with her fingers in her lap as she stared at the dark, snow-covered fields out the window.

We pulled into my driveway, and I got out, opening her door for her and offering her a hand. She took it, sliding out of the seat. Closing the door behind her, I kept her hand in mine as I locked the truck and walked her up to the front door. Unlocking the door, I pulled her inside behind me, closed the door, and immediately wrapped her in my arms, her face pressed against my chest.

"I'm so sorry I wasn't there," I muttered against her hair with my hand cupping the back of her head.

"It's not your fault. It's not *anyone's* fault, Lennon," she said, looking up to find my eyes.

"I should have been there. I shouldn't have said yes to Cal, I should have stayed at my damn store. You would have been safe, Oakley. But you were fucking scared. You're *still* scared."

She shook her head. "I was just shaken up."

I looked up at the ceiling, pursing my lips tight together to keep my frustration with the whole situation at bay. She didn't need me being upset about this, but fuck, what if something had happened to her?

She reached up, setting her delicate hands on my cheeks and tugging my face down. "Look at me."

I did. I looked down, right into those green eyes full of strength and beauty and perseverance.

"I'm okay, Lennon. I'm not hurt." She grabbed my hands, sliding them to her neck, then down her chest, to her waist. "I'm not scared." Her eyes held mine, all the fear in them from when I found her in the ambulance gone. "I'm okay," she repeated.

I didn't spare a second after the word passed her lips. I bent, taking her mouth with mine, kissing her with a need I didn't know I could possess. It was like my entire body was screaming to feel her, to know she was safe, unharmed, and mine.

My feet moved until her back hit the wall of my front entry, my hands tangling in her hair, angling her head up to mine. My lungs strained for a deep breath, but I didn't need oxygen, not right now. I needed Oakley's mouth on mine, her body connected to me.

Her hands were in my hair, my hat falling to the ground behind me; they were on my neck, scratching at my skin like she couldn't get me close enough. *I* couldn't get close enough.

I reached down between us, my hand skimming her shirt across her stomach as I undid her jeans, slipping my hand into her panties. She gasped, the sound nearly bringing me to my knees.

I fucking loved when she did that.

My middle and index finger stroked circles on her clit, then moved to slide inside her, her knees buckling as I filled her tight pussy. Using my body to keep her up, my fingers moved in and out of her slowly. I didn't want her to come on my fingers. Not yet.

"Think you can keep yourself up?" I murmured against her lips.

She nodded, and I moved my other hand from her hair. Keeping my fingers inside of her, I lowered myself to my knees, pulling her jeans down to her ankles with my other hand. She stepped out of them one foot at a time, and I moved them to the side. Then I brought my mouth to her inner thigh, leaving soft kisses on her skin as I kept my fingers deep inside her, moving them slowly, not curling them yet.

Her hands found my hair as her stomach twitched with every kiss I landed on her sensitive skin. "Tell me what you want, baby," I murmured against her skin, gazing up at her from where I knelt before her.

"Your mouth," she whispered.

"What was that?" I asked, wanting to hear her demands louder.

"I want your mouth," she repeated, this time with more force behind her words.

"Good girl. Where do you want it?"

She huffed, like she didn't want to wait any longer.

Say the words and I'll do it.

"Between my legs," she instructed.

I hovered my mouth above her clit, my breath warm on her skin.

"Doing what?" I asked, keeping my eyes on hers. I was at her mercy and there wasn't anywhere else on this planet I wanted to be than kneeling before her, about to devour her.

She was staring down at me like lust had taken over completely, her eyes glazed over. "Suck on my clit, Lennon."

I smirked and wasted no time obeying. My lips closed over the bundle of nerves, sucking it into my mouth, working it as she threw her head back against the wall. Her fingers scraped at my scalp, the burn a welcome feeling as I curled my fingers inside her, finding that perfect spot.

She moaned, her knees bending slightly. My other hand reached up to flatten against her stomach, keeping her upright against the wall as I knew her orgasm was building.

I quickened the pace of my fingers inside of her as my tongue flicked her clit, and without warning, she was screaming, her pussy completely seated against my face as she tensed against the wall, her walls pulsing around my fingers.

I groaned against her and I knew in that moment there was nothing more attractive than getting the pleasure of making Oakley come. I was the one making her unravel, causing ripples of pleasure to coarse through her. It was easily my favorite activity.

As she came down from her orgasm, she slumped against the wall, her breath evening out. Sliding my fingers out of her, I slipped her panties back on her, leaving her jeans on the floor, then stood, my hands gliding up her body as I went.

Pressing my lips to her forehead, I grabbed her hand, then pulled her down the hallway to my bedroom.

"Are you hungry?" I asked her after flicking the light on.

"Kind of," she admitted, her cheeks still flushed.

I pulled back the sheets on my bed, gesturing for her to lay down. "I'll order us some pizza."

She sat on the bed, but didn't lay down as she eyed the very obvious bulge in my jeans.

Crouching before her - *this was quickly becoming my favorite thing to do around her* - I took her hands in mine. "Why don't you lay back and turn on some TV while I'm calling the pizza place?"

She eyed me. "How am I going to do that when your cock is teasing me?"

I smiled. "I can go in the other room."

She frowned. "Maybe I don't want pizza for dinner."

I chuckled, my thumb absentmindedly rubbing circles on the back of her hand. "A lot happened tonight, Oak, and I probably shouldn't have distracted you the way I did, but you're hard to resist."

"That was the best way to distract me. Believe me."

"Let's eat some food, watch some trashy reality TV show, and see how you're feeling, okay?"

Her eyes lit up. "You like trashy reality TV?"

My smile widened. "No, but I got the hunch that you do."

She tipped her nose up. "There's nothing better than watching cheesy drama between people you don't know to get your mind off the day."

"I guess we'll find out," I said as I stood.

Her jaw almost fell to the floor. "You've never watched reality TV?"

I shook my head. "Don't really have time for TV."

"Well, you're going to need to find time because you and I are going to binge Jersey Shore."

"Jersey Shore? Isn't that the one show with those Italians who just go around to clubs and yell at each other?"

She beamed up at me. "You're already more invested than I gave you credit for."

I sighed, my lips still pulled into a smile.

I didn't care what Oakley and I did, as long as it was together.

I'd watch all the trashy TV drama shows with her.

BEAT AROUND THE BUSH

Taste every inch of her while we did it, too.

30

OAKLEY

After Lennon insisted I take the day off work, we binge-watched Jersey Shore practically all day, in between us being unable to keep our hands off each other, and dropping the rental car back off at the rental place.

Leo and Jacey had covered the store yesterday, and Lennon already had a window repairman working on the front of the store, along with getting more secure locks installed. I was originally scheduled with Leo today, but Lennon had told him not to come in. He wasn't exactly happy with Leo right now, but he also wanted to give him a break after he'd been covering so much the past few days.

The conversation between the two of them was inevitable, but I hoped the time in between the break-in and their talk would help Lennon calm down a bit. He was as hard as stone when he called Leo yesterday morning to ask him to cover our shifts with Jacey. He was holding back what he really wanted to say, waiting to do it in person.

I didn't blame Leo for what happened, and I knew Lennon didn't either, but if Leo had been at the store like he should have been, Lennon may not be so worked up over it. Although, I was coming to find that Lennon didn't like the idea of me being put in harm's way regardless of who I was with or where I was.

Lennon was signing the paperwork for the repair on the window when the bell above the door dinged.

And none other than JP walked in.

He approached the register like he was in a hurry, his eyes searching what was visible of my body behind the register. "Are you okay? I heard about the break-in, but you weren't here yesterday."

I gave a closed-lip smile, his concern for me slightly off-putting. The entire break-in was embarrassing to talk about in itself. I didn't love expressing how scared I felt during the whole thing, even to Lennon. "I'm okay."

JP's shoulders dropped an inch with the breath he released. "That's good. I thought you may have been hurt since you weren't here."

I narrowed my eyes slightly in thought. It felt like he *wanted* me to say where I was.

"I took the day off," I said simply. I wasn't about to tell this stranger that I was at my boss's house being worshiped by his tongue.

He reached into the pocket of his jacket, fishing around for something. "Well, I got you this."

My eyes followed his hand as he pulled it from his pocket, presenting a small black box.

"What is it?" I asked. The box wasn't labeled with a brand or company. It was just a black, rectangular cardboard box that fit in his palm.

He held it out to me. "Here, open it."

Furrowing my brows, I carefully plucked it from his palm, rotating the small package in my hands. Flipping the top, I looked down into it before pulling the slim metal item halfway out.

A pocket knife?

"What is this?" I asked, knowing what it was but confused why he'd given it to me.

"To protect yourself," he said, like I should've known that's what it was for.

I slipped it back into the box, having not even taken it out all the way. Holding it back out to him, I shook my head. "I can't accept this."

His forehead creased, not making a move to grab it from me. "Why not?"

"I don't want a knife. I don't have a use for it." I mean, seriously, did he think gifting a stranger a knife was some way to get into her pants? Even if that wasn't what he wanted, it's not like we knew each other outside of me selling him dog food.

He shoved his hands in his pockets, clearly not taking the box from me. "But you do have a use for it. What if someone breaks in again?"

Setting it on the counter between us, I said, "It won't happen again."

He raised an eyebrow. "You know that for sure? I mean, no one *thinks* they're going to need to defend themselves, then bam, someone's breaking into your store while you're alone."

"How'd you know I was alone?" I asked hesitantly. Maybe it was on the news that I was the only employee here at the time?

"Everything okay?" Lennon interrupted, coming up beside me.

I looked up at him, the tightness in my chest easing a fraction with his presence. "Yeah."

"What's that?" He nodded at the box sitting on the counter.

"A gift for Oakley," JP stated, frustration clear in his tone at Lennon interrupting us.

"A gift, huh?" Lennon looked down at me like he was trying to gauge if I was comfortable with this or not.

I grabbed the box, shoving it into the drawer below the register. "Yep. JP just wanted to make sure I was okay after the break-in." *And gifted me a goddamn knife to defend myself.*

Lennon moved his attention back to JP, who was shooting daggers at him. "Was there anything else I could help you with?" Possessiveness seeped into his tone, and after the other night, I didn't blame him for feeling protective.

"Nope. Have a good day, Oakley," JP said to me before he turned on his heel and strode out the door.

"Do you know him?" Lennon asked as soon as he was gone.

"No. He just comes in for dog food sometimes," I said.

"Hm," Lennon hummed in thought.

I faced him, setting my hands on his chest. "Hm, what?"

He wrapped his arms around my waist, tugging me closer. "What was the gift?"

"Something stupid that I'm just going to throw away. It was nice of him, but I really don't want it."

His brows pulled together. "Not fond of gifts?"

"Oh, I love gifts. Just not from strangers like that," I stated. I'd always dreamed of having a guy who'd bring me things like flowers or leave notes for me or take me on cute dates as a surprise. Gifts from someone you loved just felt different than gifts from a stranger. I was thankful for them regardless, but knowing your significant other thought of you enough to surprise you was so wholesome.

"What are you doing this weekend?" he asked.

I licked my lips like I was thinking about my nonexistent plans. "Hmm, that depends. Why?"

"I want to take you on a date. A proper one." His hazel eyes were clouded with hope and something like anxiety, like he was nervous about what my answer might be.

"That sounds like something I could find time for," I said with a smile.

The corners of his mouth tipped up as he leaned down to press his lips to mine softly, his tongue darting out at my lips. I welcomed him, parting my lips to let him in. Reluctantly, he pulled back. "I'll pick you up on Saturday at ten a.m."

I smiled. "It's a date."

31

LENNON

The week felt long and short at the same time, but it was finally Friday. Working in retail, Fridays lost all they were talked up to be, becoming just another day of the week for me. But this Friday in particular was one I had wanted to skip since I woke up this morning.

I'd scheduled Leo and I together today, and at the time I'd made the schedule, I had no idea I was going to have to have a conversation with him about leaving Oakley here alone the night of the break-in.

I had one rule.

Don't let anyone close alone.

You leave at the same time, together. None of this *I need to leave early, so you're going to be alone* bullshit. I understood that things came up, but at that point, you call someone else in. I don't care if it's five minutes or two hours before the store closes.

You call someone in to cover or you keep your ass here.

Leo knew this. I instilled it in him the day he started working here.

So the fact that Oakley was in danger, and he was nowhere to be found when he agreed to cover me? That wasn't going to fly.

I'd blamed myself for leaving her here, then I'd blamed Leo, and eventually, I finally came to the realization that it was no one's fault but the person that broke in. Leo being here or not would not have stopped it from happening. Or, it could have, and whoever it was that broke in had been waiting for someone to be alone here. Or they sought out Oakley on purpose.

I could run through a million scenarios and all would come back to the conclusion that regardless of how or why it happened, *Leo should have been here*.

We'd just closed and I'd already taken care of counting out the money in the register when Leo walked by my office door in the direction of the break room.

"Leo, come in here, please," I called out to him.

We'd kept it professional all shift, not bringing up the fact that he'd left early that day. But you know what? That kind of pissed me off even more. The guy hadn't apologized to me or Oakley, and that shit didn't sit right with me.

Leo came around the corner, slipping into the chair across from me. I set my elbows on my desk, casually folding my hands together. "I assume you know what I want to talk to you about."

He leaned back in the chair like this was some kind of buddy-to-buddy chat. "The other night?"

"We can call it how it is. Someone broke into the store, and you left early," I stated, keeping my tone as calm as I could, when in reality, I was doing my best to keep the rage simmering deep below at bay.

God, I'd never been so mad about something. But Oakley being in danger when no one was there to help her? That made my blood fucking boil.

He stuck an eyebrow in the air. "I'm not seeing the correlation."

I was almost struck speechless. *Almost.* "You're not seeing that you broke my one rule and one of my employees was put in danger? She was *alone*, Leo."

He gave the slightest shrug. "I did break the rule, and I do apologize for that, but I had a package I needed to send out."

It grated my fucking nerves that he was so casual about this. "I don't give a fuck about some goddamn package, Leo. You left her alone here after you agreed to cover for me, and she could have been hurt."

"But she wasn't. And she said it was okay."

Not physically, but mentally I knew it messed with her. It'd mess with anyone. Fear like that didn't just go away because you were safe now. I didn't miss her looking over her shoulder the past few days, her flinch if something fell on the floor, or her pace quickening when she went to the break room. I didn't give a damn if she said it was okay. He knew he wasn't allowed to leave anyone alone here, and he still did it.

"Get out." He was being careless, and I wouldn't put Jacey or Oakley through that. We looked out for each other; that's how it worked at Tumbleweed Feed.

"What?" he asked, blinking twice.

"I said get the fuck out."

He sat forward, confusion clear on his face. "You're firing me over something I didn't even do?"

I sat a little taller, only to get more air into my lungs to keep myself collected. "Did you forget about my one rule, Leo?"

He shook his head. "No, but Oakley being scared of some thief isn't my problem. Is this because you're sleeping with her?"

My entire body froze, my blood stopped pumping, my heart ceased beating. Anger was all that flowed through every inch of my being. "I'm only going to say it one more time. Get. The. Fuck. Out."

Leo stood, shoving back the chair as he did. "Whatever, man."

I almost wanted to laugh. *Almost.*

He turned on his heel and left, leaving me in the store alone.

At least this time, it was for good.

***

My knuckles tapped against Oakley's front door and I stood there, waiting for her to answer.

It was a sunny Saturday morning, but the chill in the air still bit at my skin. I'd told her to dress warm for what I had planned today, and seeing her outfit when she opened the door a few seconds later showed that she listened.

Oakley smiled brightly up at me and I stepped a foot over the threshold, unable to resist kissing her.

"Well, good morning to you, too," she said after I pulled away.

"Good morning. Ready to go?" I'd tried my best to sleep off my bad attitude from my conversation with Leo yesterday, but the only thing that really brightened my mood was looking forward to spending today with Oakley.

Jacey was at the feed store today with the new hire, Mateo. I'd been on the verge of hiring him when I interviewed Oakley, and no offense to Mateo, but there was no way in hell I wasn't hiring her. Now that Leo was no longer working there, it opened up the position for Mateo to fill.

He'd worked in retail before, so he knew most of the ins and outs, but Jacey was still training him on the register and everything today. I'd called him before I left the store last night, and he'd been more than happy to take the job.

Thank God for that, otherwise my date with Oakley would have taken a rain check.

"Yep, let me just grab my purse." She reached behind her to the tiny table she had by the door, then slipped out, locking it behind her. She was wearing light blue jeans with a white knitted turtleneck, her denim jacket over that, white gloves, white snow boots, and a beige beanie.

"You got thermals under those jeans?" I asked her as we walked down the tiny path to my truck.

"Yeah. I wouldn't go out without them in this cold. The sun is a liar," she joked.

She was right. It provided no warmth when it was twenty-six degrees.

"You know, I'm curious, what ever happened to my jacket you stole?"

Her jaw dropped an inch. "I did not steal it!"

"You never gave it back, so I'd consider that theft," I teased.

She closed her mouth, a small smile on her lips. "I like it."

"Yeah?" The thought of her wearing my jacket without me around did things to me that I didn't want to admit.

She nodded. "I wear it inside sometimes."

"Not outside?"

"Uh, do you know how big that thing is on me?"

I chuckled as I opened the passenger door for her. "It's cute on you."

She got in, buckling herself and setting her purse on the middle seat. "You think so?"

I hummed in agreement. "I'm glad it's not snowing today. It would've ruined my plans."

"What might those plans be?"

I leaned in with a hand on the door frame above me, my lips hovering over hers. "You'll just have to wait and see."

Her lips tipped up and I pressed my mouth to hers, never able to get enough of her now that I'd had a taste of her. I was half tempted to say "screw the plans, let's just lay in bed all day," but I promised her a date.

I closed her door and rounded the truck to get in, then pulled onto the road, heading for the ranch. I wasn't sure if Oakley knew how to ride, but I guessed I'd find out in about thirty minutes.

Guiding the truck up my parents' driveway, I pulled to a stop in front of the white barn and killed the engine.

"A date at your parents' house?" Oakley teased, a smirk pulling at her mouth.

I shook my head, cracking a smile as I got out and came around to hold her door open for her. "I guess it is my parents' place, isn't it?"

She slid out, fixing her jacket as I closed the door. Callan was in the covered arena teaching a lesson when he waved over at us. After waving back, I took her hand in mine, leading her through the large open door of the barn.

"Are we mucking stalls on our first date?" she asked, peering at Red, who stuck his head out of his stall as we passed.

"Wouldn't that be romantic?" I said sarcastically. "Know how to ride?"

She halted in her tracks, pulling me to a stop with her. "Ride?"

"Yeah, a horse."

"No... I don't," she admitted, sounding a bit defeated.

"I'll teach you," I offered, hoping she'd say yes.

"Today?" she squeaked.

I nodded. "Yes, today, Oakley."

"But there's snow," she pointed out.

I glanced to my left, looking out the door, then back at her. "We have an arena."

She looked behind her like she could see it. "But Cal's using it."

"He'll be done by the time we're tacked up. Come on." I grabbed her hand, leading her to a small palomino mare's stall. "This is Butterscotch."

Oakley reached up with a gloved hand to pat her muzzle. "Hi, Butterscotch."

The cold had the apples of Oakley's cheeks a light shade of pink, a pop of color with her red hair against her light outfit. "Cal uses her for lessons for young kids. She'll take care of you."

Oakley had this look on her face as she pet the horse that made me melt right where I was standing, despite the freezing temperatures. She was all affection and admiration for this thousand-pound animal enjoying the scratches she was giving. Being around Butterscotch made her worries instantly ease away, like a weight was lifted off her shoulders.

This was exactly what she needed after the week she'd had.

"Ready to get her saddled up?" I asked, hating to interrupt the moment she was having. Cal needed the arena for his lessons, but he was giving me an hour in between them to do this with her, and I didn't want to waste a second of it.

"Yeah." She kept her gaze on the horse for a moment before lowering her hand and stepping back.

Grabbing the rope halter off the stall, I unlatched the gate and slid it open. "Let's get her halter on."

I stepped into Butterscotch's stall and slid the noseband over her muzzle, then situated the poll strap behind her ears. "People can get this backwards, but I always tell myself to make a D towards the butt, then pull it through the D." She watched as I pulled on the end, tightening the knot.

I handed her the lead rope, then stepped out of the stall, giving them space. She walked out behind me, the mare following her. "We'll just take her over to the cross ties and do the rest."

Oakley and Butterscotch followed me over, then I helped secure her in the ties before showing Oakley how to put on her tack. Once the horse was saddled, I quickly got Winston ready, then we headed for the covered arena where Callan was exiting with his student.

"Good luck, Oakley," Cal said to her as he passed us. "Lennon's not the best teacher."

I hit him on the shoulder. "Better than you."

"Callan's the best horse teacher ever," the little boy perched on the lesson horse defended.

I held my gloved hands in the air in surrender, the rein dangling from my thumb. "Sorry, Captain. You're right. Cal here's the best."

The boy looked triumphant, like he knew Callan was a one-of-a-kind teacher. It was true - he was. He had a special touch with kids - always had.

Callan and his student headed toward the barn to untack while Oakley and I entered the arena. We headed towards the middle of the open space and came to a stop, my boots digging into the sand.

Looping the reins over Winston's neck, I left him to stand there while I approached Oakley, who was visually measuring how she was going to get her leg in the stirrup. "I'll help you," I offered.

"I'm not *that* short," she pouted.

I looked down at her with a frown. "You're pretty short, Oak."

She placed her hands on her hips. "You're just abnormally tall, and so is this horse."

"She's fourteen hands," I pointed out.

Oakley's brows furrowed. "I don't know what that means."

"She's short," I stated.

Oakley glared up at me. "Do you have something against short people?"

I shook my head, blowing air out of my nose. "I think I *have* something for short people. A short redhead, in particular."

"Well, this short redhead doesn't appreciate you pointing out her flaws."

"Flaws?" There wasn't a single flaw on Oakley, not in my eyes.

She dropped her hands to her sides. "I've been made fun of a lot for my size."

My hand grabbed her waist, spinning her to face me. "Want me to kill them?"

She huffed. "You can't just kill people, Lennon."

I shrugged. "I can if they upset you."

She waved a hand in the air. "It was a long time ago, in high school."

"That's not a long time ago for you," I pointed out. About six years ago for her, if I was doing my math right.

"Are you going to get me on this horse or are we going to keep pointing shit out about me?"

Sassy. I liked it.

In one swift motion, I lifted her by her waist into the air, plopping her down in the saddle.

Her jaw dropped. "Lennon Bronson!"

I grabbed the reins from Butterscotch's neck, handing them to her. "I was just helping you," I said innocently.

She took the reins from me and I set one hand on her outer thigh, the other on the horse's shoulder. "How am I going to learn to do it by myself if you manhandle me like that?" she asked.

I raised a brow. "Don't like when I manhandle you?"

She frowned. "Well, yes, but–"

"Then I'll keep doing it."

Her cheeks flushed and my hand slid a bit higher. She was barely a head taller than me on Butterscotch, placing me eye level with her shoulder. "Ready to ride, Oak?"

But fuck, I wished she was riding me instead.

She held her chin high. "Ready."

Sliding my hand down her leg, I placed one tiny snow boot into the stirrup, thankful they weren't those massive, bulky snow boots people liked to wear. They were small and cute, just like her. She looked down at her other leg, fixing her foot in herself.

"That length okay for you?" I asked.

She pursed her lips, and I knew she wasn't thinking about the stirrup. Neither was I.

"Perfect," she said with a small nod, looking down at me with a slight glaze over her eyes that screamed need.

"Let's get to it, then."

32

OAKLEY

We rode around the arena for about an hour while we talked about my family and his childhood on the ranch. Lennon stayed by my side the entire time on Winston, listening to every word I said. His horse was a mammoth in comparison to Butterscotch, but it wasn't anything new having to look up at Lennon.

My insecurity had just slipped out when Lennon was talking about the horse being short. I'd always hated how short I was, but ever since I met Lennon, I didn't mind it as much. The way my cheek pressed against his chest or how his chin rested on top of my head when we hugged.

Then finding out he liked our height difference? It was like all insecurities about it went out the window. And I know, they say you shouldn't rely on a guy to make you feel good or happy, but if being with Lennon made me feel more confident in myself, I didn't see why it was such a problem. Isn't that what relationships should be? Lifting the other up?

Lennon lifted me up, mentally *and* physically. Into the saddle and through the clouds. Is that where the saying *on cloud nine* came from? Because that's where I was when I was around Lennon.

He had helped me take Butterscotch's tack off, putting the saddle away for me along with his own. I ran my hand along Winston's neck, admiring his coat. Lennon had said he was a bay dun, but regardless of what he was, he was beautiful with his two-toned mane and stripe down his back.

"I'll just put the horses back and we can continue on our date," Lennon said, coming out of the tack room.

"That wasn't the whole date?" I questioned. What else did he have planned besides riding?

He shook his head, unlatching Winston and Butterscotch from the cross ties. "Just getting started. I'll be right back."

Lennon headed down the walkway with both horses following behind him, their hooves clomping on the ground echoing throughout the barn. I walked over to the tack room, taking in the wall of saddles and various other pieces of tack hanging from hooks. To the left was rows of extra saddle pads, and directly next to the door was a bulletin board with random notes and a few photos of the Bronson family.

Bailey was in every photo, right in between Reed and Lettie in each one. In the ones of them posing, everyone had a giant smile on their faces, but in the few that were taken off guard without everyone in them, you could tell the dynamic between each person.

There was a photo of Bailey smiling down at Lettie as she scowled at Reed, one of Callan grinning next to a student perched on a pony, another with Lennon on his horse beside his father, and one of their mother standing beside the banner for Bottom of the Buckle Horse Rescue.

Strong arms wrapped around my waist from behind as Lennon nuzzled his nose into the side of my neck. "Whatcha looking at?"

My head tilted, giving him more access to my neck. His breath caused goosebumps to travel up my spine as his lips lightly brushed my skin. "I want to help with the rescue."

I spun around in his arms, angling my head up at him.

"You do, huh?" he asked.

I nodded. "I think I like horses."

He smiled. "I hope you do. There's no getting away from them in my world."

"I might just like them a little more when you're riding them," I confessed. He did look downright drool-worthy in the saddle. Not that he didn't on the ground, or in bed. There was just something about a cowboy on his horse that did it for the female population, and I was quickly becoming a part of the majority in this.

Cowboys were fucking sexy.

He tucked my hair behind my ear, then cupped my cheek, stroking his thumb along my skin. "We can come out to the rescue any day you want."

Perching up on my tip toes, I pressed my lips to his, getting lost in him. His hand slid through my hair, cupping the back of my head to pull me closer to him.

A throat cleared to the left of us, interrupting our kiss. "I've got a student coming in ten, so no sex in the barn."

Lennon pulled back, keeping his eyes on me as he said, "Don't worry about it, Cal. We were just about to take it somewhere else."

"Did not need to know that," Cal muttered under his breath as he disappeared into one of the horse's stalls.

"You ready to continue our date?" Lennon asked.

I nodded, and he grabbed my hand, leading me out to his truck.

***

There was a big basket sitting on the middle seat of Lennon's truck as he drove up a muddy road. It looked freshly plowed, the snow piling up on the sides of the trail.

"Where are we going?" I asked for the third time.

"Just because it's been five minutes doesn't mean I'm going to tell you," Lennon pointed out.

I pouted in my seat, watching the hilly terrain pass by out my window. There were mountains in the distance right on the horizon, towering over the hills before them. Bottom of the Buckle Ranch was nestled in the foothills. The house, barns, and arenas were built on the flat piece of the property, but the rest was smooth hills that led into the mountains.

Idaho was beautiful. This part of the country was like no other. It could go from miles and miles of flat land, then all of a sudden, a mountain would sprout up thirteen thousand feet in elevation.

The truck jostled with each bump we ran over in the mud. "Did you talk with Leo yesterday?" I asked Lennon.

He hesitated, adjusting his grip on the wheel. "Yeah, I did."

"Did he apologize?"

Lennon's tongue pressed into the side of his cheek. "He did."

I watched his demeanor shift. "What aren't you telling me?"

He sighed. "I fired him."

I opened and closed my mouth, trying to figure out what to say to that. "You did what?"

"I fired him," he stated calmly, like it was just another Friday for him.

"Why?" My voice rose in pitch. I couldn't help but feel like Lennon firing him was my fault.

Lennon glanced over at me, his face serious. "You were scared, Oakley. You were at the store alone, and you could have been hurt."

"Did you really need to fire him?"

There was something he wasn't telling me. There had to be.

"Yes."

I stared at him a few moments longer, then turned my gaze out the windshield as we crested the hill. There was no point dwelling on it. What's done was done.

He turned his truck around at the top, backing the bed closer to the edge of the hill before he turned it off.

"Stay in here," he instructed, opening his door and grabbing the basket off the seat, taking it out with him.

The truck shifted slightly as he hopped into the bed, but I kept my gaze in front of me, staring out at the barns in the distance. They were tiny specks now, showing just how big their property really was.

A few minutes later, he opened my passenger door. "Ready."

I tried to hide my smile. "Ready for what?"

"Why don't you come see?" He reached in, grabbing my hand to help me out.

He closed the door behind me and covered my eyes from behind. "No peeking."

"Yes, boss," I teased.

He led me, instructing me where to put my feet, then had me stop and turn. His hands fell, and I took in the sight before me.

He'd laid a massive blanket out in his truck bed, complete with pillows, two more blankets, and a small wicker basket filled with what I presumed was food. There were little white flowers scattered all over the blanket with a few roses throughout, battery-powered candles propped on the sides of the bed, and a big thermos next to the basket.

"Lennon..." I started.

"Yeah, Oak?" He was watching me admire the setup.

"This is..." Thoughtful? Beautiful? There were no words to show my appreciation and how it made my heart melt. No guy had ever done something like this for me before. It was always takeout and a movie. Never a cute setup with an entire day planned out.

"Come on," he said instead, seeing that I was speechless. He stepped in front of me, facing me as he set both hands on my waist. In one swift motion, he was lifting me and propping me on the tailgate.

We were almost eye level now, and as much as I loved the gesture behind me, all my attention was on Lennon.

"Did you plow the trail just for this?" I asked.

He shook his head. "Bailey did. He's the one who told me about this spot."

"I guess I'll have to thank him, then," I said.

He put a hand over his heart. "Not me?"

I shrugged. "It seems like Bailey did a lot of work here..." I teased.

He crawled up on the tailgate, gently guiding me so I was laying on my back. I laughed as he kissed my neck, his cold nose tickling my skin while his fingers dug into my sides in an attempt to tickle me through my sweater and coat.

"Okay, okay! I surrender! I'll thank you!" I managed to get out between my laughs.

He lifted his head slightly, looking down at me with so much admiration in his eyes, it made my throat tighten.

"I should be thanking you," he said.

"Why?"

He brushed a stray strand of hair off my forehead. "You make waking up every morning something to look forward to. I used to not be able to wait to get off work and get home to be alone, but ever since you walked through that door at Tumbleweed Feed, all I look forward to is going *to* work to see *you*. My entire mind is images of your smile, your red hair, your green eyes, your laugh. God, Oakley, I love your laugh. It brightens a room more than the sun can even dream of doing. I can't help but smile when I hear it. And I guess what I'm trying to get at, Oak," he shifts a bit higher, hovering over me, "is that I would love nothing more in this world than to be your boyfriend, and hopefully one day something more. Would you be with me? Be my girlfriend?"

I nodded, blinking away the tears pooling in my eyes. One slipped out the corner, but he gently brushed it away with his thumb.

"Why are you crying?" he asked, concern filling his features.

I sniffled. "I didn't think coming here would have ever made me feel like this."

"Feel like what?"

"Like this is my home. *You're* my home. I was so scared when I left Colorado, thinking I'd never find somewhere that felt like I was all put together again. After my parents separated, my world fell apart. But Lennon, *you* put it back together. My entire universe feels whole again because of you."

He swallowed hard, but instead of a verbal response, he gave me all the reassurance I needed. He kissed me, sealing us together in this moment, in this life. Boyfriend, girlfriend. Husband, wife. The titles didn't matter. I used to think that they did, but Lennon was more than just a single word to me. He was my safe space, my protector, my sexy cowboy, my boss, but most important of all, he was mine.

Lennon Bronson was all mine.

He came up for air, looking down at me. "I might have to fire you," he teased.

I frowned. "And why's that?"

"I'm not going to be able to keep my hands off of you at work," he admitted.

I let out a small laugh. "Like you've been able to before?"

He tossed his head side to side, thinking about it. "I guess you're right. Maybe I should put a bed in my office."

I shook my head. "I think I like you bending me over your desk better."

He smirked down at me, pure need shining in his eyes. "I think I do, too."

33

LENNON

A week later, I made good on my promise to Oakley. I'd scheduled our days off to line up this week so we could have a day to help out at Bottom of the Buckle Horse Rescue. My mom was more than thrilled to hear that Oakley wanted to know more about the rescue, and even more ecstatic over the fact that she was now my girlfriend.

"You two are just adorable together." My mom beamed at me and Oakley in the kitchen. "I knew Lennon would come to his senses with you."

"How sweet," Reed said dryly as he came in from outside, sliding behind our mom to grab a water from the fridge.

Dad followed in behind him, setting his dark brown cowboy hat on the hat rack by the front entry. "Don't shit on everyone else's day because yours is bad," Dad grumbled to Reed.

"What's wrong with you?" I asked Reed, who was chugging the water like he wished it was whiskey. Mom didn't take too kindly to day drinking, but guarantee, he'd have that whiskey at five o'clock on the dot tonight.

"Nothing," Reed mumbled in between sips.

"Lettie was out squealing in the barn with Brandy about some guy Brandy went on a date with," Dad filled in.

Mom gave Reed a hesitant look, probably trying to weigh how much it affected him.

"Oh, yeah. He's a really nice guy," Oakley piped in. Reed turned his attention to her as she spoke. "They were talking about him in the group text last night before she left. She sent a whole bunch of outfit options, and settled on this-"

"Sounds like she had a good time," I interrupted. Oakley was good at rambling, and I could tell she was nervous. Reed had that effect on people when he got that murderous look in his eye. Not that he wanted to hurt Oakley, but probably the guy who Brandy went out with.

"Anyway, we're going to head out to the barn, get started on some stuff," I told my mom.

"Can you work on cleaning the water buckets and filling them?" Mom asked, slipping into her authoritative tone she spoke in anytime it came to the rescue.

"Yep. We'll do those first." I grabbed Oakley's gloved hand, leading her outside and away from pissed-off Reed.

"Sorry he's such an ass," I apologized as we headed down the porch steps.

"He's a little scary," she admitted.

I sighed. "Really?" The last thing I wanted was for her to be scared of my brother.

She laughed. "No, Lennon. He's not. He's just scared to admit his feelings."

I eyed her as we walked hand in hand through the crisp morning air. "What feelings might those be?"

She shrugged. "I'm not one to say."

"What's that mean?" I asked as we entered the barn.

"There's a history there, right?"

I nodded.

"Well, he obviously doesn't hate her," she said.

I scoffed. "If there's one thing I know for certain about Reed and Brandy, it's that they cannot stand each other."

"Has he ever told you why?" she asked, curious.

"No. Has Brandy told you?"

She shook her head as I grabbed two scrubbing sponges from the shelf by the meds room. "No. She hasn't told Lettie, either."

Oakley took one of the sponges from me. "I wouldn't worry yourself with those two," I said. "It's pointless trying to figure them out."

She looked around us at the stalls, seeming to drop the subject. "So tell me how to do this."

"Well, my mom's got a certain way she likes it done. Empty the water outside of the barn. That part is important because you don't want their shavings all wet. Then scrub any algae out, rinse really well, and fill them back up. We do it a few times a week."

She smiled. "Where do we start?"

***

An hour later, we were on the last stall. Oakley was braiding the horse's mane while I stood by the bucket, making sure the hose didn't slide out.

"You're very lucky, you know," Oakley said, glancing over her shoulder at me and taking account of my backwards hat for the tenth time.

"I know," I admitted, taking her in. She was so peaceful, her delicate fingers spinning the dark hairs, looping them over each other.

She frowned, sensing I wasn't thinking about the ranch. "For growing up on a ranch."

"I'm lucky for a lot of things in this life, Oak." One of those things being her.

I could list all the things I was grateful for, but my mind would always go back to her.

Checking the water line, I kinked the hose. "Ready when you are."

She finished off the braid she was working on, patting the horse's neck before slipping past me out of the stall. I followed, closing the gate behind me. Before she could continue down the aisle, I looped an arm around her waist, pulling her back to my chest.

"Where are you off to so fast?" I murmured in her ear.

"Turning off the water?" she said, her statement sounding more like a question.

"Hey, Cal!" I called out, knowing he was done with his lesson.

"Yeah?" Callan called back from somewhere in the barn.

"Mind turning off the water for me?"

"On it," he responded. A few seconds later, the pressure on the hose loosened. I dropped it, the remaining water seeping out in the aisle.

"What are you..." Oakley stated, but before she could finish, I scooped her up in my arms, carrying her into the med room.

I kicked the door shut behind me, setting her on her feet. Reaching behind me, I swiftly locked the door, then pinned her with a look, unable to help my eyes from drifting down her body.

"What are you doing?" she demanded, confusion seeping into her voice.

"Taking what's mine, baby."

I backed her toward the wall, then lowered myself to my knees, keeping my eyes on her. She swallowed audibly, green flames of desire blazing in her eyes.

"I can't keep my hands off you, Oak. Your pussy is my only craving, the thing I've dreamt about every night since I first had a taste. I want nothing more than to kneel before you and worship your sweet, pretty pussy."

My hands trailed up the sides of her thighs, sliding to the front once they hit her hips, my fingers working to undo her pants.

"What about the door?" she asked, her voice more breath than anything.

"Locked it," I muttered.

Tugging her jeans down, I left them around her ankles, her knee-high socks on display.

"Fuck, Oak. If it wasn't so cold, I'd have you bare, but I can't fucking wait." My voice was hoarse with anticipation and need.

She stared down at me as I moved her panties to the side, exposing her slick pussy. She was already wet, and I wondered how long she'd been thinking of me.

"So fucking perfect, Oakley. All of you. There isn't an inch of you I don't want to touch, not a sliver of skin I don't want to taste."

Unable to resist her a second longer, I dragged my tongue up her center, eliciting a gasp from her lips. My tongue flicked over her clit before my mouth closed around it, sucking on the sweet bundle of nerves. She let out a quiet moan, and I groaned, popping my mouth off her.

"No holding back."

Her eyes were glazed over as she stared down at me. "But-"

I shook my head, slipping a finger into her before she could get another word out, which caused her mouth to fall open.

"He's gone. I want to hear you scream." Cal was done with lessons for the day, so she had nothing to worry about.

Bringing my mouth back between her legs, I licked, sucked, flicked, and added a second finger, pumping her in a steady rhythm, the tips of my fingers grazing over her sweet spot deep within.

Her breath quickened, her head falling back against the wall with another moan, this time louder.

"That's what I like to hear from my good girl. Now how can I make you scream?" I stared up at her, marveling at the column of her exposed throat, her red hair cascading over her shoulders as her breasts rose and fell with each breath.

"Like this?" I added a third finger and she gasped, another moan slipping past her lips.

"Hmm, that won't do. I want it louder," I said before stopping, my fingers deep inside her, hooking them right against that spot.

"Like that, Oak?"

She nodded quickly, her eyes squeezing shut as she began to ride my hand.

Her core tightened, and I brought my mouth back down over her clit, sucking it into my mouth, the tip of my tongue flicking over the bundle.

Her hand gripped the top of my hat, the other grabbing for something to hold onto on the wall.

And then she ignited, her entire body spasming, her legs threatening to give out on her as she came, her pussy pulsing around my fingers. I groaned against her as she screamed my name, her moans filling the small room we were locked in.

Releasing her clit, I watched as she came down, then slowly slid my fingers from her, all three digits dripping. She peeled her eyes open, watching me as I slipped them into my mouth, tasting her on me.

She was so fucking sweet; I couldn't get enough of her.

"Turn around," I ordered as I stood.

"What?"

"You heard me, baby. Turn around." I *needed* to be inside her. Needed to feel her slickness drenching me.

She faced the wall, and I set my hands on her hips, dragging her ass back toward me. "Hands on the wall. Ass up."

Oakley placed her palms flat on the wood wall, bending at the waist so her ass was on full display for me.

Fucking hell.

I could come in my goddamn pants just *looking* at her.

I was a thirty-two-year-old man about to have an orgasm in my jeans just seeing Oakley exposed for me.

"You okay, baby?"

She nodded, her hair falling over her shoulder. "I'd be better if you were inside me."

I let out a groan as I got to work on my pants. "That's my girl."

Sliding my jeans and underwear down my thighs, I gripped my shaft, pumping a few times to alleviate some of the pressure in my cock, then lined the tip up with her entrance. She was still soaked, the remnants of her orgasm glistening in the light.

"Please," she begged, perking her ass up even higher.

Grabbing her hip with one hand, I slowly pressed into her with ease. I watched as I slid in to the hilt, my fingers digging into her skin.

I stayed deep inside her and she pulsed. "Oakley," I warned.

"I don't think I'm going to last long," she said, her hands trying to grip onto the wall.

"Then don't, baby. Let it out."

I slid out, then began gentle thrusts, making sure I hit deep every time.

"Lennon," she whimpered.

I placed a hand on her lower back, applying the slightest pressure to get her at the perfect angle.

And then her legs clenched, right along with her pussy, and I was in *fucking heaven*.

My core tightened and I let out a moan as we came together. Instead of pulling out this time, I emptied into her, feeling her pulse around me as I stayed so fucking deep inside her.

Nothing on this planet felt better than this. Better than Oakley wrapped around me.

After she caught her breath and I was sure we were both done, I slowly slid out of her. I watched as some of my release dripped out of her, but instead of cleaning her up, I situated her panties, then helped pull up her jeans.

"I need to go take care of this," she said after turning around, waving her hands in front of her thighs.

I shook my head as I pulled up my pants and buttoned them, then pinned her with my eyes. "Not happening."

Confusion marred her features. "What do you mean?"

I backed her up a few inches until her back hit the wall, then placed my hands on either side of her head, palms flat on the wood. "You're going to walk around with our mess between your legs like the good girl I know you are, and once we're done in this barn, we'll go home."

She arched a brow. "Do I get to clean up then?"

"We'll take a bath, and I'll scrub every inch of your body. Then after, I'll rub your feet, maybe play with your hair."

Her eyes narrowed slightly. "Why?"

"I want to take care of my girl."

Her gaze darted between my eyes, like she was searching for something. Whatever it was, she wasn't going to find it. I was being honest.

"Okay," she said.

I cupped her face in my hands, pressing a soft kiss to her mouth, then one to her forehead.

"Now let's get back to work."

Oakley was all mine, and I didn't think I'd ever get used to the feeling of that.

34

Lennon

Winston trotted circles around me in the round pen, working out his energy before I decided to get on him. The winter weather always made him grouchy, and I really wasn't in the mood to battle him today.

In the covered arena to my left, Callan was teaching a lesson to one of his students. The teen seemed to know the basics, but Callan was working on getting him more comfortable in a lope.

The sun was beating down, reflecting off the snow still clinging to the ground around the ranch. It was bitter cold, so I wasn't planning to work Winston too hard. The last thing I wanted was him getting cold from sweating too much.

Easing him into a walk, I let him cool down a bit as Callan exited the arena with his student.

"Hey, why don't you go untack and I'll meet you in the barn?" Cal told the boy.

"Yes, sir," the boy said, giving me a nod in hello as he passed.

Callan approached the round pen, resting a boot on the bottom of the fence.

"Having fun?" Cal asked.

I shrugged, bringing Winston to a stop with a low, "Woah."

I turned to Cal, letting Winston do his own thing. "Beats being at the store."

Cal's brows pinched a bit. "Not loving work anymore?"

I shook my head, kicking at the dirt. "It's not that."

He draped his arms over the top of the fence as I approached him. "Talk to me."

Wrapping a gloved hand over the cool metal, my eyes drifted off to the pasture beyond the barn. "Would it be weird if I said I found something else to love, and that makes the store less enjoyable?"

"Some*thing* else or some*one*?" he asked.

I pinned him with a look. "Does it matter?"

He dropped his boot back to the ground. "I know the feeling, Len."

And he was right. He did.

He'd been in a position before where someone wanted him to make a choice, and he chose the ranch. Not because he didn't love her, though. It was just the healthier option.

He pulled his gloves off, stuffing them in his coat pockets. "There's a way to divide your time between the two and still be happy, you know. You don't have to put all of yourself into just one thing. Plus, you've got the upper hand here. She works with you."

Air blew through my nose on a small chuckle. "Yeah, I guess I can work her and the store at the same time."

He pulled back. "Okay. Did not need to know that, man. I know we're brothers and all, but–"

I smacked him on the shoulder lightly. "I'm just kidding, Cal. Didn't know you were such a prude."

He set a hand over his heart, feigning hurt. "I am *not* a prude."

"I'm pretty sure going this long without sex makes you a prude," I pointed out.

He wiped his hands on his jeans, shaking his head at the ground. "This is why I don't share about my sex life."

"Why? 'Cause there's not one to share?"

He punched me in the shoulder, a bit harder than I had, but I probably deserved it.

My phone rang from my pocket, and I pulled a glove off, fishing my phone out.

"It's the leasing company," I told Cal.

"Take it. I have to go wrap up with Ben anyway. Beers later?"

I nodded. "Your place?"

"Yep. I'll text you when I'm done with lessons," he said before walking off in the direction of the barn.

Tapping the green circle, I brought the phone to my ear. "This is Lennon."

"Lennon, this is Alfred. I was talking with my colleague here, and we're open to negotiating for you to buy out your lease and purchase the property."

I froze for a full five seconds, then checked the caller ID to make sure this wasn't a prank call. Bringing the phone back to my ear, I cleared my throat and said, "That sounds great. Can you send me an email with the details?"

"Yep. I'll send it over within the hour. Give me a call if you have any questions."

"Thank you," I said to him before we said our goodbyes.

I stared at the black screen on my phone for a minute, thinking it was too good to be true, and I hadn't even seen the offer yet.

If this went through, the store would officially be mine. It wouldn't just be my name on my employees' paychecks anymore, but my name on the building, too. After all this time, they were finally willing to give in to my request of purchasing the property.

All I wanted to do right now was tell Oakley and celebrate the possibility of me owning the place.

"What's got your face all shell-shocked?" a familiar deep voice asked from the right of me.

Turning to look at him, I smiled at Beckham. "I didn't know you were here today."

Beck shrugged. "I like surprises. Why're you looking at your phone like that? Oakley sending you nudes?"

I pocketed my phone with a chuckle. "No. If she was, I wouldn't be standing out in this round pen freezing my ass off. The leasing company may let me purchase the Tumbleweed Feed building from them."

His eyebrows shot up, a big grin spreading his lips. "That's great news, Len!"

I smiled. "It is. But I don't want to get ahead of myself. I haven't seen their offer yet."

He waved me off. "Whatever it is, we still need to celebrate. Watering Hole tonight?"

"I don't know, Beck–"

"Come on. All of us at the bar, just like old times. We don't all have enough nights together anymore. Even if it's not a celebration, just come to hang out with your brothers," he practically begged.

"Fine, but I'm inviting Oakley."

He held his hands out wide. "The more the merrier."

***

I swung by Oakley's house after she got off work and dropped her car at home, then drove us to Outlaw's Watering Hole to meet with Callan, Beckham, Reed, Bailey, Lettie, and Brandy.

The neon sign outside the bar illuminated the snow falling from the sky. The clouds had come out of nowhere, bringing inches of snow that clung to the ground.

I helped Oakley out of her coat, draping it over the back of a chair by the pool table, our usual spot here at the Watering Hole. Cal and Beck were deep in a game of pool while Bailey, Lettie, and Brandy hung out by the bar, nursing their drinks.

"Want a drink?" I asked Oakley as she stuffed her gloves in the pocket of her coat over the chair.

"I can get it. What would you like?" She was looking over to where Lettie and Brandy were. I didn't blame her for wanting a little girl time.

"Beer is fine, baby. Thank you," I said before pressing a kiss to her temple.

"Be right back." She gave me a quick smile and then headed toward the bar, crossing behind the rows of line dancers two-stepping to some pop country song.

I made sure she made it to the three of them, then turned to Reed, who was sitting at the table watching Cal and Beck's game.

"How's work?" I asked him as I took a seat.

"Same old shit. Asshole horses and oblivious owners," Reed grumbled.

A lot of the horse owners in Bell Buckle knew what they were doing and trained their horses well, but there were always the preppy ones who thought their horses could do no wrong and never worked with them. Reed had been broadening his clients to get his name out there, which meant working with tricky horses and even trickier owners.

"Any of them knock the grumpy out of you yet?" I joked.

He shook his head, a slight smile curling the edges of his mouth. "What about you, asshole? How's work?"

Good ol' affectionate Reed.

"Got an offer to buy the building today," I told him.

I'd viewed the file once it came through, and they were cutting me a hell of a deal. I almost thought it was fake.

He faced me, brows raised. "Really? That's good, man. I'm happy for you."

"What're we happy about?" Beck asked, coming over with Cal, cues in hand.

"The offer," I reminded him.

Beck stuck a finger out at me. "That's right! Good terms, then, I take it?"

I nodded as Oakley and the other three approached, beverages in hand. "I almost wonder if they're tricking me into something."

"Mold in the walls?" Beck wondered out loud.

I shook my head. "No, it can't be that. I know that building like the back of my hand, and they haven't been there recently enough to evaluate it like that."

Callan took the beer Bailey had outstretched to him. "Maybe they're just desperate for money," Cal said.

I chewed on the inside of my lip, thinking. "Maybe. But then why cut the price so low?"

Oakley handed me a beer, sipping on her own before saying, "They probably just came to their senses and realized you deserve it."

"Yeah, Len. Don't think too far into it. Take it for what it is and sign the damn paperwork before they take back their offer," Beck said.

Reed crossed his arms over his chest, settling back in his seat. "It's what you want, isn't it?"

I looked to Oakley, who was waiting for my answer. I'd told her on the way over, and she was ecstatic to hear the news. She knew I'd been wanting this for a long time, and it was finally happening. Tumbleweed Feed would finally officially be mine.

Setting my beer on the table beside me, I looped an arm around her waist, pulling her closer to my side. "It is what I want."

"Mom can take a look at the contract if you're worried," Cal offered.

I nodded once. "I'll swing by the ranch tomorrow and see what she thinks."

"And even if it's not the deal you want to sign on, you can still negotiate," Beck said.

"Either way, we're really happy for you, Len," Lettie piped in, sensing the stress I was under from the whole thing.

I smiled over at her. "Thanks, Lettie."

She gave a smile, pressing into Bailey's side as his hand idly rubbed up and down her waist from where his arm was wrapped around her.

I looked at Oakley, who was watching as everyone got lost in side conversations. "How was work today?"

Her eyes met mine over the rim of her beer as she took a sip, then set it on the table beside me. "It was good. Pretty busy because the sun was out. Jacey and I kept everything under control, though."

I brushed a strand of hair off her forehead, the rest of the bar drowning out as all my focus was on her. "That's good. I'm glad I'll be there with you tomorrow."

"Miss me?" she asked with a quirk of her lips.

Bringing my hand around the back of her head, I brought her closer so my lips grazed her ear. "I missed everything about you, Oak. Especially that little gasp you make when I fuck you."

Her lips parted as a breath of air escaped her. With her body facing away from them, her hips hidden from view from everyone, my hand trailed between her legs, feeling her warmth seeping through her jeans.

"I bet you're wet already, aren't you?" I whispered in her ear.

She nodded, a small whimper passing her lips as my thumb pressed where her clit was hidden under the fabric.

I pulled my hand away, turning her around to sit her on my leg. My hands bracketed her hips as I brought my lips to the shell of her ear. "I guess you'll have to be a good girl and wait until we get home."

She pressed her lips together, giving a tight nod as her hips rocked slightly on my leg. My fingers dug into her hips, anchoring her in place. "That little move is going to get you in trouble, Oak."

Her cheeks flushed, bringing out her freckles. She turned her head slightly and said, "Maybe I like trouble."

And then we sat there until everyone was ready to go home.

That short drive to my house was the longest it'd ever been with the temptation to pull over and take Oakley right then and there. But she was in trouble, and I was going to deliver.

35

OAKLEY

Lennon and I walked quietly up to his front door. I walked under his arm as he held the door open for me, and before I could make it another step past the threshold, he grabbed my arm, spinning me around and pinning me up against the now-closed front door.

He had his hands pressed against the door on either side of my head, caging me in. "Do you think I forgot your little move at the bar?"

I shook my head.

"Use your words like a good girl, Oak, and maybe I'll forget what you did."

But I didn't want him to forget. I *wanted* him to punish me.

He traced my chin with a finger, then circled my lips. "Open," he commanded.

My lips parted, my tongue laid out for him. He inserted his finger, and before he could command further, I closed my lips around it, sucking it while I twirled my tongue around the end.

He slid his finger deeper, and my tongue flexed as he hit my gag reflex.

A devilish glint shone in his eyes at my small gag and he pulled his finger out with a pop.

"On your knees," he instructed.

I lowered myself to my knees, keeping my eyes on his, despite his cock bulging against his jeans right in front of me. His tongue did a slow pass over his bottom lip as he admired me before him.

His face was all hunger and need, like he wanted more from me.

Whatever it was, I'd give it to him. I'd do anything for him.

"Take your shirt off," he commanded.

I sat up on my knees, pulling my coat off, then my shirt, tossing them to the ground.

Without moving his gaze from mine, he said, "Pull your bra down."

I reached for the straps, but before my fingers could loop around them, he grabbed my chin, forcing me to keep my eyes on him. "Not the straps, Oakley. The cups. Pull them down. I want to see those tits on display when you choke on my cock."

I swallowed, my throat burning for the sensation of him in my mouth. He kept his hand on my chin as I pulled the cups of my bra down, my breasts spilling out, looking full and round.

"That's my good girl. Maybe I'll go easier on you since you're listening so well," he said, his voice hoarse.

I bit my lower lip and he straightened, looking down at me.

"Take my cock out, baby."

I reached for his zipper, sliding it down slowly, then tugged his pants down with his boxers, his cock springing free.

As my eyes bored up at him, I wrapped my hand around it, pumping it twice, then parted my lips. His hand fisted in my hair and held my head in place.

"Tongue out," he said.

My tongue laid out past my lips, but he shook his head. "Farther."

I did so, sticking it out as far as it would go.

"I'll do the work, baby. You just keep that pretty mouth how it is."

I blinked up at him in response, and he gripped my hair harder, the slight burn turning to pleasure as my core heated. My mouth was salivating for him, eager to have him fill me. Dropping my hand from his cock, he wrapped his own around it, gliding the tip along my outstretched tongue.

Once it was glistening with my saliva, Lennon thrust into my mouth slowly, going further until I gagged slightly, my eyes watering.

"Deep breaths, Oak. You're taking all of it tonight, whether you choke or not."

I breathed through my nose as he kept his cock still, then once my reflex settled, he slid further, his cock sliding down my throat.

"Just like that, baby. Breathe in and out. That's all you have to do. I'll do the rest."

Once he was fully inside my mouth, my eyes watered more as he slid out all the way, my mouth instantly missing him filling me.

"Do you like my cock down your throat, baby?"

I nodded, keeping my tongue out like he wanted.

He slid back in, and once he hit my gag reflex, my tongue twitched again. "No more taking it easy. I told you you were in trouble. Now I'm here to punish my girl."

He seated himself down my throat as I choked on him. My tongue flexed along his length, eliciting a moan from him as I swallowed his cock. He pulled out quick, then shoved back in as I evened my breathing out through my nose, calming my reflex.

"That's a good girl. Learning how to take my cock in all your holes."

I moaned at the thought of him filling me elsewhere, but my moan was cut off by him shoving back down my throat, fucking my mouth relentlessly. I reached up to cup his balls, and he moaned, his head falling back as I made sounds around his cock I never thought I'd hear come from me.

His hand tightened in my hair. "Can I come in your pretty mouth, baby?"

I gave a hum in response along with a slight nod, and in seconds, warm spurts of his release were shooting down my throat. I swallowed each drop as he came, and once he was done, he pulled his cock out of my mouth, hauling me up under my arms.

He pressed his mouth to mine, kissing me like I was his only source of oxygen.

"You're so fucking perfect, Oakley," he murmured as he fixed my bra.

"What about me?" I asked. My panties were beyond soaked, and I was sure there was a wet spot on my jeans.

He tucked my hair behind my ear. "Baby girl, my punishment didn't just end with fucking your throat. We're going to go watch a movie, and I'll think about letting you come after."

My bottom lip pouted out, and he kissed it, dragging my lip in between his teeth with a small bite.

He pulled back and smoothed a hand over my hair, then bent to hand me my shirt.

Lennon Bronson was torturing me, but I liked it.

I liked everything he did to me.

36

OAKLEY

Lennon had stuck to his word, keeping me practically squirming on the couch with my legs draped over him as we watched our movie. Once the movie was done, before the end credits could even begin rolling, he'd scooped me up in his arms and brought me to the bedroom where he'd made me come over and over again, telling me how much of a good girl I was for waiting.

Before Lennon, my sex life was more boring than a twelve-hour car ride with no music and nothing but flat desert terrain to look at. I'd had orgasms before, but nothing like what Lennon made me experience. Lennon didn't just unravel me - he made me explode every time an earth-shattering orgasm overtook me.

The bell dinging above the door pulled me from my thoughts, and I looked up to find Margaret walking through the door to Tumbleweed Feed with a small cart in front of her. She was leaning some of her weight on it to keep her steady.

"Good morning, Margaret. You doing okay?" I asked her, eyeing the cart.

She nodded, waving me off with a wrinkled hand. "I'm alright, dear. Just got my cart with me today for all the bird seed I have to buy."

I gave a closed-lip smile, coming around the register. "Let me help you pile it in."

She didn't fight me this time. "That'd be lovely."

I kept a slow pace beside her as we made our way down the small animal aisle, coming up on the bird seed stacked neatly on the shelf. "How many bags?" I asked her.

"Four, please," she replied, her voice scratchy with age.

I picked up two at a time, loading them into her small cart. "You must have lots of new birds coming around."

She adjusted her grip on the handle of the cart, watching as I loaded the bags. "Oh, yes. I've been getting a lot of finches coming around, mingling with my sparrows and robins. I've seen a few starlings, too. They're beautiful. And have you ever seen a mountain bluebird? I thought blue jays were pretty, but those ones have them beat."

She rambled on about all the birds visiting her bird feeders lined up outside and which ones loved which bird baths as we made our way back to the register. I scanned one bag, entering a quantity of four into the register, then read off her total. Her hand shook slightly as she inserted her credit card, then pulled it out when the machine beeped at her.

Handing her the receipt, I said, "I can help you load these into your car."

"I don't want to trouble you," she said hesitantly.

"No trouble at all, Margaret. As you can see, we aren't too busy today." I rounded the register, holding the door to the store open for her. She walked past me, and I resumed my slow pace next to her as we headed for her car.

"This one's mine," she said as we came to a stop behind a gray sedan. She began fishing for her keys in her purse, muttering to herself how she needs to keep better track of them in the black hole that was her handbag.

As I waited, my gaze landed on Lennon at the side of the store, loading hay bales into one of the locals' truck beds. The muscles under his flannel strained as he loaded them. Even being this far couldn't hide his solid form.

He tossed another bale in the bed and caught me staring, flashing me a smile with his hat backwards. My cheeks flushed and I hoped he couldn't see them from where he was.

"Ah, here they are," Margaret announced, beeping the locks on her car and popping the trunk.

I forced my gaze away from Lennon and back to Margaret. Opening the trunk the rest of the way, I began loading the bags of bird seed, but the last one caught on the edge of the cart and ripped open.

I covered the hole with my hand before too much could spill out, setting it back in the cart positioned in a way that the seed would stop flowing out of the hole.

"I'm so sorry, Marg. Let me get some tape for this. I'll be right back," I told her before I rushed back inside the store to get tape from Lennon's office.

Rifling through the drawers in his desk, I found a roll sitting atop a paper with a small note scrawled on it. My name was printed on the top of the folded paper. Furrowing my brows, I picked up the paper, unfolding it.

Lennon must have stowed my resume paper in here after our interview and forgot it was here. My eyes fell to the bottom of the page where he'd written a short note.

Stop getting lost in her eyes and pay attention to her damn answers.

I bit into my bottom lip, remembering watching him scribbling something down and worried he was disappointed in my responses. But he hadn't been disappointed. He'd been besotted. With me.

Swallowing a gulp, I folded the paper and shoved it in my back pocket, making sure to grab the tape. As I made my way back through the store, I grabbed another bag of bird seed to make up for the bit that spilled on the ground.

"Sorry about that, Margaret," I said as I set the spare bag in her trunk and taped up the hole on the other bag. "Keep both. I feel bad for ripping the bag."

She watched as I set the ripped bag in her car. "Don't worry about it, dear. The birds out here will love the spilled seed. Keep that other bag, I didn't pay for it."

"You lost some on the ground, and I don't want to upset your birds at home."

Margaret gave me a sweet smile, her thin lips pulling tight. "You're too sweet. I'll let the birds know it came from you."

I closed her trunk gently. "Thank you. Want me to help you put the cart away?"

She waved me off again. "I'm old, but I can still do *some* things by myself. You've done enough. Have a nice day, Oakley. And tell Lennon I said hi," she added with a wink.

I smiled. The people in this town didn't miss a thing. "I will. Drive safe, okay?"

"Always do," she said before coming up to the back door of her car and folding the cart up to stow away in the back seat.

I watched her drive out of the parking lot, then headed over to where Lennon was finishing up loading the hay bales.

"Hey," I said, looking up to him. He was standing in the truck bed, arranging the bales.

"Hey to you. Margaret doing okay?" he asked, wiping a bit of sweat from his brow despite the cold temperature.

"Yeah, she is." I gnawed on my bottom lip, watching his gloved hands wrap around the bailing twine as he picked up the bales and plopped them down in an order that would allow him to fit the most in the bed of the truck.

"So I was in your office..." I started.

He glanced at me, raising an eyebrow before continuing on his work. "You have fun?" he joked.

I frowned before pulling my resume out of the back pocket of my jeans. "Found this."

He straightened, heaving a breath as he eyed what was in my hand. "What's that?"

"Lost in my eyes?" I teased with a small smile.

Realization dawned on him and he took his hat off, running a gloved hand through his hair before plopping it back on with the bill still backwards.

"Yeah, uh…" He seemed to be at a loss for words.

"You've liked me since my interview?" I asked.

He leaned over slightly, bracing his hands on the side of the bed to peer down at me. "I've liked you since you hit my truck."

"But you didn't know me," I pointed out.

He shrugged, pressing his lips together. "No, but I heard your voice, and something about you just drew me in from the beginning."

My cheeks flushed again, a blush blooming against my freckles. "I really thought you hated me."

"I could never hate you, Oak. Even if you wrecked my ol' K15."

My brows lowered. "I did *not* wreck it."

"Sorry, you're right. You wrecked *your* car."

I frowned right as he bent to press a quick kiss to my lips.

"I think you were made for me," he said, a big grin spread across his mouth.

I set my hands on my hips, the paper pinched in between my fingers. "Oh, really?"

He stood straight so that I had to angle my head back further. "Yeah. And I was made for you."

And then he went back to stacking the bales, and I knew in my heart he was right.

As much as I hated the circumstances that brought me to Bell Buckle, I loved the life I'd built here in such a short time.

The beginning of a life with Lennon Bronson.

37

OAKLEY

"I'm still surprised you were able to lock Lennon down," Jacey said as she filled the dog treat container on the counter by the register.

"Honestly, me too," I replied as I faced the shelf closest to the front of the store. "I really thought he hated me for hitting his truck."

She closed up the box of dog treats, stowing the spares under the register. "He comes off as a grump sometimes, but he never means any harm by it. I think Reed rubs off on him sometimes."

I laughed at that. "Out of all of the Bronsons, Reed tops the grump scale for sure. Speaking of the Bronsons, I'm hanging out with Lettie and Brandy tonight at Lettie's place if you want to come?"

"That'd be fun. Thank you."

The bell above the door tinkled and I turned to greet the customer, but as soon as I saw who it was, the words tumbled out of my mouth.

My dad was standing there in a button-down with ironed slacks, staring at me while I stood frozen with my hand held above a bag.

"Oakley," he started.

"Dad..." The word was barely a whisper. "What are you... What are you doing here?"

My dad looked around from where he stood, taking note of the store. "I came to talk to you."

"You came all the way to Bell Buckle just to *talk* to me?"

His eyes landed back on me, my arm now lowered to my side. "You're my daughter, Oakley. I wanted to make sure you were okay. You weren't texting-"

"Dad, this is Jacey, my coworker," I interrupted. We didn't need to have a heart to heart in front of her.

My dad looked at Jacey like he was just now noticing she was here, standing midway between us behind the register.

"Hi, Mr. Rae," she greeted awkwardly.

"Hello, Jacey. Nice to meet one of my daughter's coworkers. And see the place she's working at for the first time. Oh, and the town she's now living in," my dad said, with a little more annoyance behind the words than he should have for showing up here unannounced.

"If you guys want to talk, you can use the office. I'll just close up the store in five minutes and be out of your hair..." Jacey offered hesitantly.

I swallowed, trying to ease the frustration from my voice. "Sure. Thanks, Jacey. Dad, let's go."

I gave Jacey an apologetic look before turning on my heel and walking to the back, my dad on my heels.

As soon as we entered the office and I had the door closed, I whirled on him. "What are you doing here?"

His shoulders fell slightly, like the tension was easing at seeing that his little girl was okay. "I want you to come home, Oakley."

I crossed my arms from where I stood in the middle of the office. "We've talked about this. No."

He let out a sigh as his eyes trailed to the ground. After a few seconds of silence, he lifted his head. "Your mother and I made up."

My brows furrowed in confusion. "Made up? Like, got back together?"

He shook his head. "I don't think I can get back together with your mother after what she did to me, but we're being civil about things now. Making it a clean divorce, no drama. We just want our little girl back home."

I dropped my arms, coming around the back of the desk to plop down in the chair. I stared at the keyboard, letting all the possible scenarios run through my head.

"I can't just leave Bell Buckle, Dad," I said.

"Why?" He took a seat in the chair on the other side of the desk.

"Because there are people relying on me here."

"Like who? This little hillbilly shop needs you?"

My spine straightened. "They're not hillbillies."

He shook his head, clearing the word from his tongue. "Then who, Oakley?"

"My boss," I spit out.

His forehead creased. "I'm sure your boss can hire someone-"

"He's my boyfriend," I said, the words spilling from my tongue before I could stop them. Admitting it out loud to him was scary, but it also felt good.

My dad froze, his eyes trained on me. "Your boss... is your boyfriend?"

I nodded. "Yes."

"And that's why you want to stay in this middle-of-nowhere town? Because of some guy?"

I pressed my lips together. He wouldn't understand. He was going through a divorce with the woman who was supposed to be by his side through everything. Of course he wouldn't understand why I'd want to stay.

Heaving a sigh, I stood from the chair. "I'm not leaving Bell Buckle, Dad."

A light knock tapped on the door, and Jacey peered in with the till in her hand. "Do you want me to count this out or..."

"I can do it." I walked around the desk, grabbing the register till from her. "Sorry, Jacey. If you want to get out of here, you can. You don't have to wait for me."

"I'll just take care of some things in the back. Come get me when you're ready to leave," she said.

"Okay. Thanks."

She nodded and headed down the hall.

Setting the till on the desk, I stayed standing as I looked at my dad in the chair. "Can we talk about this later?"

"I have a meeting in Denver I need to get back for in the morning, so I'm taking the redeye out of here tonight." He stood from the chair, straightening his shirt. "I have an extra ticket if you're willing to leave."

"I'm *not* leaving!" What was so hard to understand about that? My life in Denver was just getting by. It was okay, but it didn't make me feel how I felt here in Bell Buckle. How I felt when I was with Lennon. I wouldn't trade what I had here for settling back in my old life. In the beginning, I might have, but somewhere along the way, I'd changed my mind.

He seemed taken aback by my outburst, and I was sure he was. It was rare that I spoke up for myself, but not because he forced me to cower. I just didn't like hurting people's feelings by telling them things they may not want to hear because I felt a certain way. But I was done being quiet. The only way I'd be happy was if I finally stood up for myself and what I wanted.

Something changed in me the day I left Denver, and whatever this new bravery was that I felt was exactly what I needed. It'd been missing my whole life, and I found it here.

"Is this really what you want?" he asked quietly.

My eyes welled with tears, but I refused to let them fall. "It is."

He swallowed, his Adam's apple bobbing with the action. Just that small movement showed a speck of acceptance, like he was finally understanding that I was serious in my decision. "If you want to talk further, you can call me. I'm sorry you're not happy with me right now, Oakley."

"It's not that. I'm happy here. Don't get me wrong, I was happy in Denver, too, but this is different. Bell Buckle feels like home."

His face softened as he did his best to understand. He came around the desk, pulling me against his chest. "I love you, Oakley. All a dad wants is for his daughter to be happy, and if you're happy here, then I just have to accept that. But please know that you can come back to Denver anytime. You'll always have a room with me or your mom."

I nodded as he let me go. "Thanks, Dad. I love you, too."

"You're going to be the one to tell your mother, though. Not me."

I smiled. "That's fine with me. Let me walk you out so I can finish closing."

I led him to the front of the store and unlocked the door to hold it open for him. "Let me know when you get home safe," I told him.

"I will. You be safe, too, okay?"

"Always am."

"Love you, Oakley," my dad said with a small smile.

"Love you, too, Dad."

I watched as he got in his rental car in the parking lot, pulling out of the lot with his headlights illuminating the falling snow.

A small part of me hurt as I watched him leave, but I wouldn't mistake that with thinking I made the wrong choice. Bell Buckle was right for me. Denver was in my past, the place that I grew up, but that didn't mean I had to stay there forever to appease everyone else.

My life was *mine*, and not everyone had to agree with my choices.

Closing the door, I headed back through the store to the office. I shut the door behind me and sat behind the desk to count out the money and finish the end-of-the-night duties on the computer.

As I was exiting out of the browser, the office door opened.

"Almost done," I said without looking up.

But instead of Jacey replying, it was a man's voice. "Take as long as you need because I'm going to do the same."

My eyes shot up, landing on JP's smirk as he closed the office door behind him. The expression on his face was anything but sweet. I scooted the chair back a few inches, like that could give me the space I needed from him.

"We're closed, JP," I said, doing my best to keep my voice steady.

"I know. Six o'clock every night."

My heart was pounding in my ears with the uncertainty of why he was here.

"And don't worry about your coworker. My friend has her locked in the stock room, but she probably doesn't know it yet."

I internally cursed, hoping she'd figure it out sooner than later and call for help. He was giving me the creeps, standing there with that look on his face, like his intentions with being here were anything but innocent.

"If you want to buy something-"

"I can't buy this, Oakley," he interrupted as he slowly walked closer to me.

"Buy what?" I asked, confused by what he meant.

"Your affection," he stated.

Unease twisted my stomach as fear froze me in place.

My affection? He wanted me to like him?

"Look, I think you're cool, JP, but-"

"Where's the knife?" he asked, ignoring me.

I searched around in my brain for what he meant.

"Knife...?"

His eyes scanned the desk. "The pocketknife. The one I gave you as a gift to protect yourself. Where is it?"

I thought back, trying to remember where I'd stashed it.

The register.

It was in the front of the store.

If he'd let me go get it, I could slip out the front and call for help for Jacey.

"It's up at the register. I can go grab it if you let me."

JP shook his head, coming around the side of the desk. I stood, inching myself backwards to put distance between us.

"Should've kept it with you, Oakley. You never know when you'll need protection. Why don't we play with mine instead?"

He reached into his pocket, pulling out a pocket knife that was a few inches longer than the one he'd given me. He spun it in his hand, admiring it.

"I feel like you didn't appreciate my gift," he said.

My back hit the wall and I tensed. "I did. I just leave it up there because that's where we're most likely to get robbed."

His eyes pinned me. "But the thief didn't steal from the register, did he? He stole from the shelves."

My brows pulled together. "How did you know that?"

The items stolen during the break-in weren't public record.

He shrugged. "I know a lot of things."

Realization dawned on me. "It was you, wasn't it?"

The corner of his mouth lifted. "Ding, ding, ding."

"But why? Why break into a feed store?"

"I wanted the shiny new toy in town. And I would have been successful if you hadn't called the cops so quick."

I couldn't help the shiver in my bones. "You don't want this, JP. What if you go to jail? What about your puppy?" I was using anything I could to get him to reconsider whatever his plan was.

He took one giant step, placing himself directly in front of me, and slammed his hands into the wall beside my head. "There's no fucking dog! And there's no chance I'm going to jail. You'll be out of here before anyone knows something is up. Now shut your mouth. I want to play."

38

LENNON

I'd read over the contract probably forty times at this point, highlighting the important bits, the numbers, the logistics. As far as my mom and I could find, there was nothing screaming a red flag at us. It was all perfect.

Beckham sat at the island across from me while Mom cleaned up from dinner. "If you keep staring at the damn paper, it's going to burst into flames," Beckham said.

I shot a glare at Beck from where I stood, my hands braced on the island on either side of the paper.

"It's a big decision, Beckham. Give him a break," Mom chimed behind me.

Beck shrugged. "I didn't even read the contract for the circuit. I just signed, and off I went."

"Oh, so it wasn't all the horses bucking you off that made you dumb, you're just naturally that way?" I joked.

Mom smacked my shoulder with a dish towel as Beck laughed. Growing up, we all teased each other relentlessly and I missed that with Beck being gone so often.

It wasn't like staring at the contract was going to suddenly make anything pop up on the page that told me not to sign, so I grabbed the pen, scribbling my name down on the line at the bottom with today's date.

Something so simple to solidify something so big.

"Oh, shit," Beck murmured, watching me sign.

I tossed the pen down on the counter, taking a step back.

Mom peered around me to look at the paper, then erupted in a shriek. "Lennon, you did it!" She wrapped her arms around me from behind, squeezing me hard with the dish towel still clutched in her hand.

I smiled, staring down at the still-wet ink of my name. "It's officially mine."

"Well, not until you give it to the leasing company," Beck pointed out, like the smart-ass he is.

I glared at him and he pressed his lips together with a shrug and an eyebrow raise.

Mom dropped her arms from around me, spinning me around to look up at me. "I'm so proud of you, honey."

"Thanks, Mom."

"Are you going to tell Oakley?" she asked.

"Of course I'm going to tell Oakley. I think she's hanging out with Lettie and Brandy tonight, though, so I'll wait to tell her tomorrow."

My phone rang from the pocket of my sweatshirt and I pulled it out, seeing Jacey's caller ID lit up on the screen.

"I'll be right back," I told the two of them as I walked out onto the front porch.

I tapped the green dot to answer and brought the phone to my ear. "Hey, Jacey. What's up?"

"Someone locked me in the stock room and I don't know where Oakley is," she said hurriedly, her voice full of panic.

"What? Do you have a key?"

"No, it was up at the register because I was waiting for Oakley and her dad to finish talking before we left."

"Her dad was there?" A million possibilities ran through my head. I didn't know every detail about her and her dad, but I knew he wanted her to go back to Denver. What if he took her? Oakley wouldn't have left to go to Lettie's house after work if she wasn't sure where Jacey was.

"They were talking in the office. It seemed heated, but I've been yelling for Oakley and I don't know if she can't hear me or what, but she hasn't come to get me."

I cursed under my breath, shoving my way through the front door, back into my parents' house. "I'll be there soon, okay? Call the police and keep them on the phone with you."

I pulled my cowboy hat off the hook and crossed the kitchen to grab my keys off the island.

"Okay. Hurry, Lennon. Please," she begged, a fear I'd never heard from Jacey clear in her voice.

"I am, Jacey. Hold tight."

"What's wrong?" Beck asked, standing from his seat. I wasn't sure where our mom went, but it was best not to worry her.

"Jacey's locked in the stock room at the store and she doesn't know where Oakley is."

"I'll come with you," Beck said, grabbing his coat off the hook on the wall.

I shook my head. "Stay here in case Oakley shows up, okay? I don't know if she's at the store or…" I trailed off.

"Or what, Len?" Beck pressed.

"Her dad was there and I don't know what his intentions were."

His brows pulled together. "What do you mean?"

"It's a long story, but he wanted her to go back to Denver and she didn't want to. I have to go."

He sucked in a breath as the worst probably flew through his mind. "Okay. Be safe," he said, his face hard as stone as I hurried out the door.

I tried calling Oakley as I rushed to my truck, but it went straight to voicemail.

As soon as I was in the driver's seat and heading down the driveway, my phone rang. I hit answer without seeing who it was, setting it on the seat beside me.

"Have you heard from Oakley?" Lettie asked through the speaker.

"Why? Has she called you?" My foot was like a brick on the gas as I sped down the main road toward town.

"No. That's why I'm calling you. She was supposed to come over tonight, but she's almost an hour late."

"I'll let you know if I hear from her," I said, having to bite my tongue from adding anything else. I didn't want Lettie to worry, and I especially didn't want her to get involved if anything had happened to Oakley.

"What's wrong?" she asked. She must've heard something in my tone.

"Is Bailey with you?" I asked her.

"Yeah... Lennon, what's going on?"

I sighed, then took a turn faster than anyone should. "I don't know where Oakley is or if she's okay. I'm going to find her."

"Find her?" Alarm crept into Lettie's tone. "What do you mean find her?"

"She was closing with Jacey and someone locked Jacey in the back. No one can find Oakley."

"Oh my God," she whispered into the phone right as I took the turn into town.

"I'm almost to the store, Lettie. Just stay home and I'll call you with an update once I have one. She's fine," I said, but I wasn't sure if I was saying it to reassure Lettie or myself.

"Okay. Be safe. Please. I love you," she said as Bailey asked what was wrong in the background.

"Love you, too, sis. Everything is okay. I have to hang up now."

"Okay," she whispered.

I hung up the phone, leaving it on the seat beside me as I sped into the parking lot of Tumbleweed Feed. Taking up three spaces, I yanked my keys out of the ignition and got out of the truck, closing the door behind me.

I looked through the window by the front door to see if anyone was inside, but from what I could see, there wasn't a soul in the store. If Oakley was in there, she'd have to be in the office or the break room. I tried the handle, but it was locked. Using my key to unlock it, I pushed the door gently in an attempt to not make the bell tinkle.

Softly closing it behind me, I quietly made my way to the stockroom, unlocking the door.

"Jacey?" I called out in a whisper.

"Len!" she whisper-shouted back, jumping up from where she was perched atop a short stack of dog food and running over to me. She threw her arms around me, mumbling her thanks into my shirt.

"Have you heard from Oakley since our call?" I asked her.

She shook her head at the same time a voice piped up from her phone perched on the bags of kibble.

"Is everything okay?" a woman asked.

"It's the 9-1-1 operator. They're on the way," Jacey told me before going back over to her phone. "Everything's okay. My boss is here now."

The operator was quiet for a moment, seemingly not happy that there was yet another person here possibly being put in danger.

"I'm going to go find Oakley," I told Jacey.

"Everyone needs to stay put until police get there. They'll find your friend," the woman said.

"Sorry, ma'am, no can do. I have to find my girl. I hope you understand that," I said before heading out of the stock room.

I kept my steps quiet as I made my way toward the hallway that led to the office. The store was silent until I rounded the corner, then muffled voices floated down the hall. I couldn't make out what they were saying, but it was definitely Oakley and some man.

"Late night?" a voice called from behind me.

I swiveled to find Leo standing in the aisle about ten feet from me. "Leo? What are you doing here?"

He chuckled, the sound digging into every nerve-ending in my body. This wasn't right.

"Taking care of business. Isn't that what you'd always say to me when I'd ask what you were doing all those hours in the back office instead of being on the floor?"

My eyes caught on a glint of metal from the waistband of his pants, and with a quick glance, I saw he had a gun tucked there. I took a step away from the hallway, toward Leo. "That's why I hired extra help, Leo."

He scoffed. "Please. You only hired her to sleep with her. You know, I thought we were cool, Lennon, and then you had to go and fire me." He smiled wide, a hysterical laugh bursting out of him. "Over a girl!"

My skin grew hot with the anger that surged through me. "Don't involve Oakley in this."

"I mean, isn't she why you fired me? Wasn't that the whole reason?" He stalked forward a few steps, prowling like a lion about to pounce. "Because your poor girl was in danger for a few minutes?"

"It was because you broke my one rule. We went over this."

"You see, I have a hard time believing that."

I held my ground, doing all I could not to turn around and go to Oakley. Leo was getting in my way. "What's the plan here, Leo?"

He shrugged, the act casual. "Revenge."

My heart skipped a beat as a loud thump from the office echoed down the hall. "Who's in there with her?"

Leo grinned, and I wanted to wipe the look off his fucking face. "My friend." In one swift movement, he had the gun in his hand. He twisted it around, admiring it.

"Come on, Leo. Put the gun down. You're really going to do this over a *retail* position?"

He looked at me, his eyes frantic. "Where the fuck else am I supposed to work in this small town? The goddamn junk yard?"

It was an option.

"Just put the gun down and we can talk, okay?"

"No!" Leo's voice echoed through the store, bouncing off the linoleum floors.

He raised the gun, aiming the barrel at me. "I'm done fucking talking. You didn't want to hear what I had to say when you fired me, so I'm not giving you the choice. You've said all you need to say."

He cocked the gun, but before his finger could pull the trigger, a blur of movement moved behind him and then Leo collapsed.

My eyes moved from Leo to Beckham, who stood poised above him with a shotgun in his hand.

"Beckham?"

"I could've shot him, but I figured knocking him out was the safer route," Beckham said, heaving a breath.

I should've been relieved, but I wasn't. Not with Oakley still in that office.

"Beck-"

"Go get your girl. I'll watch him until police show up."

They should be here any minute now, but I couldn't wait. I had to get to her.

I gave a quick nod and spun, aiming for the hallway. Creeping closer to the door, I tried the handle, but it was locked. As I gently slid my key into the slot, the man's voice became clearer.

"I can bring you to my house. Teach you to ski."

"I don't want skiing lessons, JP. I already told you this," Oakley said, her voice small as she tried to keep her tone gentle.

"But I want to give them to you, and what I say goes," he said, right as the lock clicked. I paused, but the sound of his footsteps didn't falter as he paced the room.

Twisting the handle, I braced myself for what was to come. I wanted to take him off guard; make sure he didn't see me coming so he wouldn't have a chance to hurt Oakley.

Her safety was my number one priority.

"But don't you want me happy?" Oakley croaked.

Two big footfalls, and then Oakley shrieked.

Without thinking, I threw open the door, seeing the man's fist curled in her hair with her head tilted back as he stared down at her. The door slammed against the wall and he twisted, keeping his grip on her hair.

And then all I saw was red.

39

OAKLEY

JP spun me, pressing my back to his chest with his hand still tight in my hair, giving me no choice but to angle my head back to try to relieve the sting on my scalp. His other hand moved, and I felt a pinch at my side.

Lennon's eyes flew to what I assumed was a knife pressed against me, and I wanted to cry at his pained expression. If I was stabbed… If I died…

"Move that hand any fucking closer to her and I swear to God, I will kill you," Lennon gritted out.

"I don't think you're in the position to make threats right now," JP retorted, and I wanted to kill him myself.

JP wanted me alive. At least, I hoped so. There wasn't much love to be had from a corpse. So I had to use that to my advantage - that hopefully, if he did injure me, he wouldn't do enough damage to kill me.

Using that information, I tried to feel where his arm was in coordination with my elbow, subtly moving my arm until I brushed his skin. If I could knock his arm away and possibly get him to lose the knife, I could get away from him.

"What do you want?" Lennon asked, though his hard tone gave the impression he had little he was willing to bargain.

"Her." Nausea cramped my stomach and I wanted to throw up.

Lennon shook his head, malice practically dripping off him. "No can do."

"You think you own her?" JP spit out.

Lennon looked at me when he spoke. "No one *owns* her. My girl makes her decisions on her own, and it looks to me like she didn't choose you."

JP's grip loosened the slightest bit at Lennon's words, and I took that as my chance. I reared my elbow back, making contact with the bend in his arm. A sharp pain bit into my side, but I ignored it, focusing on getting away from him. Metal clanged on the ground, and I knew he'd dropped the knife.

Lennon was already moving before the knife fell, grabbing JP's wrist and squeezing it hard enough that I heard a snap. JP yelled out in pain as his fist let go of my hair, and then Lennon had him slammed up against the wall, far away from me as I shrank back.

My scalp burned and the adrenaline of feeling trapped in this office with the fear that no one would come was coursing through my veins. My fingers trembled slightly as my back hit the wall behind me. I hadn't realized my body needed the support to stand as I watched Lennon punch JP in the jaw.

His fist slammed into JP's face over and over again, until blood was seeping out of his nose and mouth. Lennon's other hand was clenched in JP's hair, holding his head up. After a few more bone-shattering punches, he threw JP to the ground and turned to me.

I knew my fear was written all over my face. But it wasn't fear of Lennon. I could never be scared of him. It was the past hour that wrecked me, how JP was acting like I was going to be his. He was obsessed with me and I should have seen it from the beginning. I should have told someone. Maybe that could have prevented this from happening.

Lennon crossed to me, cupping my face and examining every inch of me. "Fuck, Oakley. You're bleeding."

I didn't care. I collapsed into him, needing his support. Needing his body against mine. He held me to his chest as my limbs shook, the adrenaline wearing off to let the panic set in. His hand fell to my side and pain shot through me.

I looked down, following his gaze. I was bleeding. *A lot.*

Footsteps sounded from the store and I tensed, but that only made the pain worse.

My mind went foggy, every noise around me muffled like I was underwater. A moment later, I was scooped up, and my head fell against a warm chest.

Lennon's chest.

We were moving, but I couldn't pinpoint where. The pain was too much. It felt like my side was torn in half, but it couldn't be that bad, right?

Lennon's movements were stiff but hurried, his grip gentle, and then cool night air wrapped around me as we must've left the building.

"She's hurt," Lennon called out.

Another voice spewed out words, but I couldn't make them out through the fog in my head.

"Stabbed in the side. I don't know how deep," Lennon answered them.

I was laid down, but all I wanted was to be back in Lennon's arms. I reached out, my arms heavy, but my hands couldn't find him.

And then my eyes fell shut, and I found him in my dreams.

40

OAKLEY

Beeps filled my ears as my eyelids cleared away the haze with each blink. Once the room cleared, I sat up, but instantly regretted it as an ache punched me in my side.

Lennon sat forward from where he was seated beside me and grabbed my hand. His other hand cupped the back of my head gently. "It's okay, Oak. You're okay."

I gently laid back on the hospital bed, looking around the room. "I'm in the hospital?" I remembered Lennon picking me up, but after that, everything got blurry.

He nodded when my eyes found his again. "The knife went in about half an inch. They gave you seven stitches."

My eyes widened. "Seven?" How bad was I hurt?

He moved his hand from the back of my head, brushing a strand of hair out of my face. "They said it should heal quick. We can leave in about twelve hours."

"How long have I been here already?" Was it even the same day?

"I haven't been keeping close track of the time, but I'd say about four hours? I think everything just tired you out. You've been sleeping and I didn't want to wake you."

It seemed everything had taken a lot out of him, too. He looked exhausted, his hair sticking up in every direction, clearly showing he'd been tugging at it.

"You can go home, get some rest-"

His gaze hardened. "I'm not leaving you, Oak."

I felt terrible that he had to go through all of this. He must have been so scared, not knowing what was going to happen. But if I was being honest, I didn't want him to leave. Lennon was the only person I wanted right now. He made me feel safe, and after all the pain that JP inflicted, safe was the only thing I wanted to feel at the moment.

"Where's JP?" I asked.

Lennon studied me for a moment, like he was gauging if he should tell me all the details while I was in the hospital. "They arrested him, but he was pretty banged up, so he's at the hospital until they can bring him in."

My hand tightened in his with the fear that he was in the same building as me. "Is he-"

"No," Lennon said with a shake of his head, his thumb caressing the back of my hand. "He's at a different hospital. I wouldn't have let them bring him here, even if they wanted to." He hesitated, making me worry.

"What is it?"

He shifted. "Leo was there."

My eyes widened. "Is he okay?"

Lennon inhaled deeply, his brows pulling together slightly. "He was a part of it."

My mind whirled, my voice catching on itself. "He- What?"

His other hand rested on my thigh, his thumb rubbing gentle circles. "He and JP were friends, I guess. They both had separate agendas, but planned it all together. JP wanted you, and Leo knew I'd come."

I shook my head. "I don't understand."

"It's okay. I haven't really fully processed it either. But what matters is that we're both okay, and they're both going to prison for a long, long time. You're safe."

Before I could respond, the door to my room creaked open and my body braced, but Lennon gave me a reassuring squeeze. "It's just the police."

I relaxed a bit with his words. How long would I react like that to a door opening and not knowing who was on the other side?

"Is everyone okay in here?" the officer asked.

Lennon nodded. "We're okay."

"I'm Officer Harris. I just need to get her statement and then I'll be out of your hair," the woman said to us.

"Can we have just a minute?" Lennon asked her.

She gave a quick nod and stepped out, leaving the door open.

Lennon looked down at me, bringing a hand up to cup my cheek. "Are you okay to answer some questions?"

I nodded, feeling my eyes glass over as emotion clogged my throat. I didn't want to relive what happened, but I knew that I had to.

"I thought I was going to lose you," he said quietly.

His admission of his fear made full tears well in my eyes, but I shook my head. "You can't get rid of me that easy."

"Easy or hard, I don't ever want to lose you. Are you sure you're okay?"

My eyelids fluttered in a poor attempt to blink the wetness away. "I'm okay."

His eyes searched mine before he leaned in to kiss me gently. He pulled back, then pressed a kiss to my forehead before turning and letting Officer Harris know she could come back in.

***

"What do you feel like for dinner?" Lennon asked as we entered his kitchen about thirteen hours later. They'd kept me to monitor everything, then released me around four p.m. the day after the incident.

I moved to slide out of my jacket, but Lennon was there in an instant, helping me out of it. He set it on the kitchen island as I replied, "Something easy."

"Pizza?"

"Pizza sounds good. Italian supreme?"

Lennon made a face. "With white sauce?"

"What's wrong with white sauce?"

He set his cowboy hat on the hook next to where he hung his keys. "Pizza should only be made with red sauce."

"Okay, fine. We can settle on half red sauce, half white sauce."

He grinned, satisfied with the compromise. "I'll call the place if you want to get into some comfier clothes."

I ran a hand up and down my arm, wanting nothing more than to get out of these jeans and into pajamas. I hadn't got much sleep in the hospital and I was exhausted, but I was starving just the same, and wanted to be as close to Lennon as I could right now.

"I'll be back out in a minute," I said, turning to head to his bedroom.

I carefully undressed, thankful the pain meds were working overtime to keep the pain out of my side. I slipped into a matching set I'd left here a couple weeks ago. It was a light pink button up top with matching sleep shorts, which paired perfectly with my wool socks. Heading back to the kitchen, I found Lennon at the island with an array of ingredients in front of him.

"Didn't you order pizza?" I asked.

He nodded. "I'm making homemade ranch."

I slowly slid onto the barstool, craning my neck slightly to look at the ingredients.

I made a face at the large containers. "Mayo, sour cream, and yogurt?"

He mixed the ingredients together in a bowl. "Don't knock it 'till you try it. It's way better than that store-bought stuff."

I pressed my lips together, adjusting myself on the stool. "I'll take your word for it."

Lennon held the spoon out to me. "Try it."

"Do I have to?"

"Come on. You'll love it, I promise."

I leaned forward slightly and took a small lick of the spoon, letting the flavors of dill and garlic dance over my tongue. "Okay, that's actually amazing."

"Way better than the bottled stuff, huh?" he asked.

I nodded. "I don't think I can ever go back to store-bought ranch now. I could eat that with a spoon."

"Okay, maybe don't do that," he said with a smile.

About twenty minutes later, the doorbell rang and Lennon walked around the island with cash in his hand. He opened the door, greeting the pizza delivery guy. After he handed him the cash and grabbed the pizza, he closed and locked the door, then walked over to the coffee table with it.

"Aren't we eating up here?" I asked him.

"Figured we could watch a movie while we ate," he said as he set the box down, then came back to the kitchen. "Will that be comfortable for you?"

"The couch sounds amazing."

He gave a small smile, despite the worry still etched onto his face. "Want anything to drink?"

"Water, please."

He gathered the drinks, ranch, and napkins, then followed me to the couch. We turned on a cheesy Hallmark Christmas movie and ate our pizza, then cuddled until the movie was over. Once the end credits began rolling, he turned off the TV, but continued to run his hands through my hair gently.

"I'm sorry I scared Jacey. I'm just so thankful that Leo didn't do anything to her. I never would've forgiven myself if he had," I said quietly, not lifting my head from his lap.

"Don't be sorry, Oak. She was just worried, but she's okay. We were all worried about you," Lennon admitted.

"It was my fault she was back there, though. My dad showed up and I didn't expect everything to unravel the way it did."

His hand continued stroking my hair, easing the burn that still lingered at the back of my scalp from where JP grabbed me. "No one could have known what those two were going to do."

"I know." I stared ahead, trying to clear the fog from my head and be in this moment with Lennon.

"What'd your dad say?" Lennon asked.

After everything that had happened, I forgot Lennon didn't know the details about my father's visit. "He and my mom made up, but they're not getting back together." I shifted, catering to my side, so I was looking up at him from where I laid. "He wants me to move back to Denver."

His movements faltered for a second, then resumed their soothing strokes. "Is that what you want?"

"No." I sat up, using my arms more so than my stomach muscles to take the pressure off my wound, then pivoted so I was facing him on the couch. "I don't want to leave you. You've made me think of Bell Buckle as a home, and though that's not what I came here for, it's what I found in you."

"I want you to stay, Oakley. But even after last night, you still want to be here?"

I grabbed his hand, intertwining my fingers with his. "Bad things happen everywhere, Lennon. What matters is how we handle those times and come out of them. Right now, all I want is to come out stronger with you by my side. Will you do that with me?"

Something like love shone in his gaze. "Of course. I'd do anything with you, Oakley Rae. Just say the words, and I'll make it happen."

I leaned forward to press my lips to his, melting into his mouth. I'd known I didn't want to leave Bell Buckle, but knowing Lennon wanted me to stay was like the cherry on top.

Pulling back, I met his gaze. "Can we go to your parents' ranch tomorrow?"

He smiled. Despite knowing I had to rest, the only place I wanted to be was there. "Anything you want to do, Oak, and we'll do it."

41

OAKLEY

Lennon pulled into the parking lot of Tumbleweed Feed, turning the truck around so we were right in the middle of the lot, facing the store.

"What are we doing here? Weren't we supposed to go to the ranch?" I asked him, confusion clear in my tone.

He killed the engine, then turned to face me from the driver's seat. "You're looking at the official new owner of the Tumbleweed Feed building."

My jaw dropped as my mind processed his words, then I flung myself at him, wrapping my arms around him with a shriek, ignoring the sharp sting of pain in my side with the movement. These pain meds were amazing. "Lennon! Why didn't you tell me last night?"

His strong arms held me close to him. "It didn't feel like the right time with everything else going on. I signed the papers right before I got the call from Jacey."

I instantly felt guilty for taking away from one of the best moments of his life. The feeling ate away at me, but I shoved it aside to celebrate the news. "I'm so happy for you."

"Thanks, Oak. I'm happy, too."

I pulled away from him, but kept my arms around his neck so I could look into his eyes. "I don't care what's going on in our lives, I want you to tell me the big news, good or bad. Nothing is more important than something like this, Lennon."

He brushed a stray hair from my forehead. "That's not true. This store will never be more important than you. No job should come before you and your safety, Oakley. You're my girlfriend, and one day you'll hopefully be more than that, so I'm making this promise now. My work will never come in between us. My home life will always be more important than my work life."

"I didn't doubt that for a second, cowboy." I crashed my mouth to his, the kiss heated and full of need. But we had somewhere to be, and we couldn't do anything while I was healing anyway, so we needed to get going.

Pulling back, I gave him a quick peck on the cheek before settling back in the passenger seat. "I'm so proud of you."

He started the truck, driving out of the parking lot in the direction of the ranch with a smile on his face.

About half an hour later, we pulled up the driveway to the Bronsons' house, parking in front of the barn. Lennon came around to open the truck door for me and I got out.

My feet had barely touched the ground when small arms wrapped around me in a tight squeeze. "I'm so glad you're okay," Lettie said.

I hugged her back as Lennon warned them about being careful with my side, and then another set of arms came around us. "We were so worried, Oakley," Brandy mumbled into my hair.

I was sandwiched between them as I heard Bailey approach from the side. "Please, no more," I begged, hoping he and Lennon didn't join in on the group hug.

"Sorry, Oakley. I was worried, too," Bailey said before wrapping his arms around us from behind Lettie, then Lennon joined from the side.

"A group hug without me?" Beck called from somewhere further away. Boots picked up their pace on the dirt, and then another body was wrapped around us in a crushing hug, swaying us side to side.

"I won't be alive if you guys keep suffocating me," I said from the center of the group.

One by one, each of them released me, taking a step back. "Glad to see you're okay, Oakley," Beck said to me.

Though he seemed relieved, there was still a tension in his shoulders, like the worry was still deep in his bones, but something told me that the lingering concern wasn't aimed toward me.

I gave him a closed-lip smile. "Thanks, Beck."

He nodded once, then Lettie was back in front of me. "Okay, enough with the guys. Let's go have some girl time."

"I think that's much needed," Brandy added.

"I'll get started on the chores in the barn if you want to tell my mom we're here," Lennon said to me.

I nodded. "I'll tell her. I'll come help in a little."

Lennon narrowed his eyes at me, not extremely happy that I wanted to help in whatever way that I could despite my injury. He bent to kiss my temple, brushing a hand over my back. "Take as much time as you need."

Lennon headed off into the barn with Beckham and Bailey as Lettie, Brandy, and I walked up the porch steps to sit on the porch swing. I waved to Charlotte through the window before sitting down next to the two of them. We swung our legs side by side, looking out at the land before us.

"I'm staying in Bell Buckle," I blurted out. I wasn't sure if anyone thought I was leaving or not, but I wanted them to know that I appreciated their friendship. That I loved them and didn't want to leave anytime soon.

Lettie laid her head on my shoulder as the swing kept rocking. "I had a feeling you would. Bell Buckle has a way of making people stay."

"I'm glad my favorite people aren't going anywhere," Brandy admitted.

Lettie lifted her head. "We're your favorite?"

Brandy nodded. "Well, and my mom. But I love you guys."

"I love you, too, Brandy," Lettie said with tears welling in her eyes.

"Me, too," I admitted. I did love them. I loved a lot about Bell Buckle, but the people in it were at the top of my list.

This was home.

42

LENNON

The cowbell above the door at Bell Buckle Brews chimed as Oakley and I walked in, the smell of coffee beans and freshly baked pastries instantly filling my nose.

"Hi, Lennon!" Avery greeted from the table she sat at by the window.

"Good morning. Your mom make her white chocolate cranberry scones this morning?" I asked, already knowing the answer with the scent that surrounded me.

Avery nodded with too much energy for this early in the morning, dropping her colored pencil on the table and ditching her drawing to skip up to the bakery case. "They're right here. Still warm, too."

"Avery, sweetie, where's my-" Sage cut off when she saw me and Oakley approaching the counter. The door to the back swung shut behind her. "Hey, you two! How is everything?"

She looked at Oakley with a bit of concern, like she wasn't sure how to tread after the incident at Tumbleweed Feed.

Oakley offered her a smile as we came to a stop in front of the register. "We're doing good. How about you?"

Sage grimaced, but quickly covered it up with a closed-lip smile. "Getting by."

I left the two of them to talk as I bent down next to Avery, who was practically drooling over the baked goods.

"Your mom being a baker gave you a pretty big sweet tooth, huh?" I asked Avery.

She nodded, turning to me with big hazel eyes. "Mom says I got it from her."

I smiled. "Must run in the family."

Her eyes dropped to the logo on my shirt, then darted to her mom. "Mom, I want a horse."

Sage stopped mid-sentence to turn her attention on Avery, sadness with a hint of exhaustion furrowing her brows. "How do you think a horse is going to fit in our house, Avery?"

Avery shrugged as I straightened. "Like how everyone else does it, I guess."

"People who live in houses like ours don't have horses," Sage told her daughter.

Avery crossed her arms. "Well, when can I get one?"

Getting the feeling that Avery was going to be disappointed with her mother's answer, given the look on Sage's face, I interrupted. "How would you feel about riding a horse?" I asked Avery.

Her eyes lit up. "Really?"

I nodded, glancing at Sage. It was clear the disappointment in her gaze wasn't aimed at her daughter, but at herself for not being able to give Avery everything she wanted. "You can come by my parents' ranch and ride one."

"Thank you, Lennon, but I can't afford that right now," Sage said.

I shook my head. "Nonsense. You're not paying for it. Consider it a thank you for how good your food is here."

"Mom! Can I please?" Avery begged.

Oakley smiled, and I knew she was hyperfocused on me interacting with Avery.

Sage chewed on her bottom lip for a moment, then sighed. "Sure, Aves. But only once."

Avery shrieked, jumping up and down. "Thank you, thank you, thank you!" She ran around the counter and wrapped her arms around her mom's waist, holding her tight.

Sage ran her hand over her daughter's hair. "You're welcome, sweetie. Now why don't you go back to your drawing so I can get Oakley and Lennon their coffees?"

"Okay." Avery sent me a big grin before skipping back over to the table she was sitting at when we walked in.

"Sorry about her," Sage said as she wiped her hands on the apron tied around her waist.

"It's no problem at all," Oakley assured her.

"Still no luck finding a babysitter?" I guessed.

"Unfortunately. It's going okay with bringing her here, but it makes it harder to do everything while I'm having to keep an eye on her," she admitted.

"I could see if my mom could help watch her some days. She's home with the rescue stuff, and I'm sure Avery would love to be around the horses," I offered.

"I'll take you up on that if I can't find anyone else. Thanks, Lennon."

"Of course."

"So what can I get you two?" Sage asked.

"I'll have an iced vanilla latte and one of those white chocolate cranberry scones, please," Oakley said.

"Make that two scones. And I'll have a black coffee," I said.

"Always so bland," Oakley teased.

I nudged her in the arm as Sage turned to start working on our order.

"That was really nice of you," Oakley said, staring up at me.

I turned to her, setting my hands on her hips to pull her closer. "Gotta stick together in this small town."

She scoffed. "Please. Just admit it's because you have a big heart."

My hands moved up and down her sides. "You brought it out in me, Oak."

Oakley smiled up at me, her cheeks turning a light shade of pink. "I'm glad I did, cowboy."

Epilogue

Lennon

Three weeks later...

"Thank God I wasn't the one who had to load all of this up in Denver," Beckham complained with a grunt as he lifted the other end of a dresser that was full of clothes. We probably should have taken the drawers out, but Beck insisted it was fine up until the point he had to lift the piece of furniture.

"It was just me and Oakley's dad doing all of it. But we worked a lot smarter than you guys," I said as Bailey walked by us balancing three boxes on top of each other.

"Do all of you like to show off?" Brandy called from the doorway to my house.

Lettie snorted. "Brandy, you should know this by now. You grew up with them."

Oakley had decided to end her lease at the small house she was staying in and move in with me since it would be cheaper overall, and there was no point for us to be living apart. We'd flown out to Denver last week and packed all of her things in a moving van to bring back here.

Her dad was nice, and after a few dinners and beers with him, he seemed to like me. The age gap threw him for a bit of a loop, but he warmed up to me. I think seeing his daughter happy made him more accepting of her moving so far away to live with a guy who was eight years older than her.

When he'd heard about the incident after he left Tumbleweed Feed that night, he'd felt guilty for not being there to protect his daughter. After Oakley told him about the rest of the night, he'd softened a bit knowing I'd been the one to get JP away from her. Though I'd technically saved her, I still lived with the guilt that she'd been hurt, but I couldn't change the past. What mattered was that she was here, alive and healthy.

We'd gone out to dinner with her mom and met her new boyfriend. They were both pleasant, but I could tell Oakley felt a little awkward being around the new boyfriend with everything going on.

I'd taken her mind off of it afterward with my tongue between her legs.

Spring was on its way, so the highways from Colorado to Idaho weren't too terrible with ice, but we kept most of our driving with the rental truck during the day to avoid the dropping temperatures at night.

Beck and I carried the dresser inside, navigating the corners of the hallway to bring it into mine and Oakley's bedroom. We'd made space before we left for Denver, so Beck and I positioned it along the wall under the TV. Taking a step back, I set my hands on my hips as I studied the dresser in our room while Beck walked behind me to head back outside for more items.

"What're you looking at?" Oakley asked as she came into the room with a bag of clothes in her hands.

Keeping my eyes on the dresser, I said, "Admiring you in my space."

"I'm over here," she pointed out.

I turned to her with a smile, dropping my hands from my hips to set them on hers. I pulled her close, staring down at her. "All of you, Oak. You're here to stay. With me."

She looped her arms around my neck, angling her head back. "I wouldn't want to be anywhere else."

"Good. I think I'll keep you." I bent to kiss her, melting into her like I always did. She smiled against my lips, her hands sliding up into my hair.

"I think I'll keep you, too," she whispered into our kiss.

Oakley Rae was a ball of sunshine, and I knew that for the rest of my days, I'd be orbiting around her. She was my world and my universe, and I wouldn't want it any other way.

THE END

ACKNOWLEDGEMENTS

The biggest thank you to you, the reader. Without your support, I wouldn't be able to keep writing and doing what I love. It blows my mind that people want to read the things that I write, so just know that each and every single one of you is appreciated from the bottom of my heart.

To my fiance, Alex. I really have no words for you. You hype me up every damn day and make me feel so important. I truly couldn't pursue this career if I didn't have you by my side. Thank you for listening to me talk about plots for hours and giving me so many ideas.

To Colter. You're my baby, my little bundle of joy. You keep me on my toes, but without you, I don't know if I ever would've had the courage to start writing. Thank you is not a big enough word to express my appreciation for how much you've changed my life. I love you more than words could ever express. Everything I do in this world is for you. Keep smiling, bubby.

To my beta readers, thank you for reading my manuscript at its imperfect state and giving me the best advice and funniest reactions. You all make me laugh with every single one of your comments, and I'm so glad I have you all on my team.

To my editor, Bobbi, thank you for putting up with me and my countless apostrophe and comma mistakes. For answering every text with my random questions, and talking plot with me about stories I shouldn't even be thinking of right now.

To my cover designer, Ali Clemons. Once again, you've made such a beautiful cover while putting up with my indecisiveness. I'll always be so grateful for you and the work that you do.

Thank you to my absolute best friend, Kate Crew, for always listening to my voice memos about plot or answering my millions of questions. You've paved the way for me as an author, and out of all of that, our friendship bloomed into something I'll cherish forever. Here's to hoping we get those nights on the porch with our glasses of wine.

To my ARC readers, you truly are the best cheerleaders an author could ever ask for. You make every release day so much fun with all of the edits you put out. Thank you for taking the time to read my book babies and leave a review. You help make all of this possible.

ABOUT THE AUTHOR

Karley Brenna lives in a tiny mountain town in the middle of nowhere out west with her fiancé, son, and herd of pets. Her hobbies include writing, reading countless books heavy on romance, and listening to country music for hours. If she's not at home, she's either at a bookstore or getting lost in the hills on horseback. To stay up to date with Karley's future projects, follow her on social media @authorkarleybrenna.

Printed in Great Britain
by Amazon